KU-730-858

THE
JAZZ
SINGERS

From Ragtime to the New Wave

Bruce Crowther & Mike Pinfold

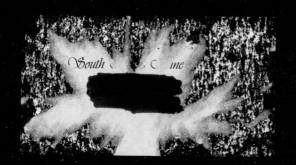

BLANDFORD PRESS
POOLE · NEW YORK · SYDNEY

First published in the UK 1986 by Blandford Press
Link House, West Street, Poole, Dorset BH15 1LL

Copyright © 1986 Bruce Crowther & Mike Pinfold

Distributed in the United States by
Sterling Publishing Co, Inc,
2 Park Avenue, New York, NY 10016

Distributed in Australia by
Capricorn Link (Australia) Pty Ltd
PO Box 665, Lane Cove, NSW 2066

British Library Cataloguing in Publication Data

Crowther, Bruce
 The jazz singers : from ragtime to the new wave.
 1. Jazz music—History and criticism
 2. Singing—History and criticism
 I. Title   II. Pinfold, Mike
 784.5   ML3506

ISBN 0 7137 1648 7

*All rights reserved. No part of this book may be
reproduced or transmitted in any form or by
any means, electronic or mechanical, including
photocopying, recording or any information storage
and retrieval system, without permission in writing
from the Publisher.*

Typeset by Graphicraft Typesetters Ltd., Hong Kong

Printed in Great Britain by Biddles Ltd., Guildford

Title spread: Memphis Slim.

WEST GLAMORGAN COUNTY LIBRARY

687023   £9.95

JULY 1986

CLASS NO 784.5

LOCATION 05

Contents

Acknowledgements

Some of the illustrations in this book come from stills issued to publicise films made or distributed by the following companies: Anglo Amalgamated, Majestic, MGM, Paramount, 20th Century Fox, Warner Bros/Seven Arts; or to publicise records made by: ABC, Atlantic, Capitol. Pictures are reproduced by courtesy of the National Film Archive London, on pages 51, 69, 81, 91, 97, 113; Phill Clarkson 3, 77; Jazz Journal International 42, 103, 107, 109, 119, 122, 164, 197; Bernard Long 135, 145, 147, 151; Harry M. Monty 177; David Redfern 199; Mike Salter 153, 193; Bruce Crowther 133, 139, 155.

All the drawings are by Mike Pinfold. Permission to quote from song lyrics has been obtained from Anglo Pic Music Co. Ltd for *Reckless Blues* by Fred Longshaw, and *Hard Time Blues* by Bessie Smith. © 1945 Bregman Vocco and Conn Inc., Chappell Music Ltd, for *Jimmy's Blues* by Jimmy Rushing; and Southern Music Publishing Co. Ltd, 8 Denmark Street, London, WC2. for *Bloodthirsty Blues, Bloodhound Blues, Moanin' the Blues* and *Garter Snake Blues*.

Instrument Abbreviations used in text

as	alto saxophone	b	bass	bars	baritone saxophone	
cl	clarinet	cnt	cornet	d	drums	g	guitar
p	piano	tb	trombone	tp	trumpet	
ts	tenor saxophone	v	violin			

6

Introduction

All music derives from song; the voice was the first instrument. Yet, in jazz, an intensely personal music, the use of the human voice has always been regarded as an anomaly, resulting in a highly vocal anti-vocalist lobby among enthusiasts of the music. There is a curious logic to this. Jazz involves improvisation, albeit built upon certain musical conventions. Singing suggests a need to adhere to certain predetermined conditions laid down by composer and lyricist. This implied inhibition of artistic imagination has resulted in singers often being summarily dismissed in otherwise comprehensive histories of jazz. This is despite their visibility and accessibility to a wider public than is usually reached by jazz instrumentalists. Thus, a singer as widely accepted as Ella Fitzgerald is often treated in jazz literature as little more than an appendage to the Chick Webb band of the 1930s. Yet, even a singer of unmistakable jazz commitment as, say, Sheila Jordan, whose integrity has prevented her from reaching the general public, is also summarily treated in otherwise comprehensive jazz books.

The idea of the singer as appendage or ornament may result from audience expectation and certain showbiz conventions which demand that the singer, out there in front of the band and in the full glare of the spotlight, should look charming and graceful and at ease. Often hidden is the considerable degree of sheer physical effort required by a singer. This, and the training and development, are no less than what is required of instrumentalists, yet the singer has to overlay it all with that patina of casual ease. It is unfair to treat singers with similarly casual dismissiveness. Or, perhaps singers have been short-changed *because* they have proved so popular with the general public? It is not uncommon for artists in many fields to meet the *cognoscenti's* grim-faced disapproval when they gain popular acclaim.

For many writers, audiences, even singers themselves, the definition of what makes a singer a *jazz* singer is only vaguely understood. When definitions are formulated they tend to be disconcertingly narrow and this usually artificial constriction nudges over the sidelines many singers of extraordinary merit. When most critics decide whether a singer is or is not a jazz singer what they in effect say is: I like to hear this singer in a jazz context, therefore this is a jazz singer; conversely: I do not like that singer within a jazz setting, therefore that is not a jazz singer. Consequently, much of the opinion expressed is primarily a matter of personal taste, greatly influenced by the nature of the singer's accompaniment, rather than a careful judgement of the singer's intrinsic qualities.

No one disputes Billie Holiday's place, few would argue against Louis Armstrong, Anita O'Day or Betty Carter. Bessie Smith, Ma Rainey and Big Bill Broonzy are rightly defined as blues singers and allocated a special but separate place. But where does this leave Ethel Waters, Peggy Lee and Ella Fitzgerald? The problems created by firm dividing lines can be immediately understood by attempting to categorise such performers as Jimmy Rushing and Helen Humes on the basis of their recordings. Now a jazz singer, next a blues singer, then maybe a rhythm-and-blues artist, sometimes a jazz-inflected singer of popular songs. Then there are singers as diverse as Mahalia Jackson and Bing Crosby. Despite their essentially non-jazz roles in the history of singing in the twentieth century, they were undoubtedly influenced by jazz and the blues; in their turn, perhaps surprisingly, they have influenced performers whose status in jazz goes unquestioned.

It is now time for all these singers, whether they perform on street corners or at Carnegie Hall, to be assessed in the same work. Thus, in this book will be found singers whose connections with the jazz world might appear tenuous, even contentious. Yet, their inclusion is justified for as those artificial divisions surrounding jazz singing are broken down, many previously unacknowledged singers can assume their rightful status in those areas of American popular music to which jazz is central.

In the following pages many singers will be discussed, some at length, others necessarily briefly. Careers will be summarised and influences considered. Most important, however, will be an assessment of the place these singers hold in the history of jazz based upon their performances.

First, however, the background against which these individual portraits are painted has to be established. This is not a history of jazz, rather it is a brief survey of its origins and, in particular, the vocal tradition in those forms of popular music from which sprang the separate strands that eventually grew so close as to be now inextricably intertwined – the blues, spirituals, ragtime and jazz and their derivatives.

1 Africa, Europe and the New World

Following the emancipation of the American Negro in 1863 a torrent of musical influences was released, changing forever the sound of popular music – first in America and eventually throughout the world. For centuries these black slaves had been isolated from their own musical heritage, while any innate musical nature some individuals might possess was repressed and their artistic talents crushed. Forcibly exposed as they were to the varied musical culture of whites, who were themselves immigrants, assimilation of alien musical traits was inevitable. Nevertheless, during the long years of slavery they retained, sometimes instinctively, often with grim and deliberate determination, many of the qualities peculiar to their African roots.

The music of black Americans, with its rhythmic complexities and unusual vocal inflections, still held distinct associations with Africa, although blurred and weakened by time and distance. The new music thus produced, although hybrid, was essentially African in both its secular and sacred forms.

In considering the African roots of black music, it is important not to rush into generalisations even though some are necessary when condensing events that ranged over centuries.

Slaves were taken from Africa over a period of several centuries, with upwards of five million being carried to the Americas. Approximately ten percent of these were brought to the southern regions of

North America – the majority coming in during the eighteenth century. Their places of origin were widespread, coming as they did from numerous different countries and cultures.

The places to which slaves were taken also differed as massive numbers were deposited among the islands of the Caribbean, and spread throughout Central and South America with a particularly large slave community developing in Brazil. Thus, the southern region of the North American continent was only one of many receiving points for slaves. Yet, no other region provided ground in which jazz grew, nor did it emerge in their African homeland. Several factors of considerable importance contributed to its development in that particular area of the New World.

As slaves had been imported into North America for more than a century before the formation of the Republic in 1776, quite clearly they did not find a unified society awaiting them. The white population was still relatively small and well-scattered. The major waves of white immigration did not occur until after the ending of the slave trade in 1808. Thus the great majority of white Americans can trace their transplanted roots back only to a time when many second and later generation blacks were already working on the plantations and farms, and in the mines and factories of the Deep South.

The white musical traditions, while generally of a common base, were varied in nature. They too came to America at different times and, most important of all, found an existing black tradition of music already re-rooted in the alien soil.

In modern times the role of the voice in European music has been overtaken by the importance of musical instruments; going back in time, however, the human voice was the major means of musical interpretation and performance in both Europe and Africa. It is not, therefore, the intrinsic differences between European and African musical traditions that are of prime importance but the point in time and space when they came together.

In Africa, the human voice has retained its original dominant status through to the present day. Musicians who play instruments are highly skilled and hold important places in tribal culture and in village and community hierarchies, which means that for most people their only musical outlet is what it has always been – the voice. Group singing was commonplace and so too was the use of song for purposes other than entertainment. Song in African nations was utilised for religious ceremonies, as hunting songs and lullabies, for education and the preservation of family and tribal histories, and as accompaniment to work. Music, and especially song, thus held an important, practical and sometimes ritual role in the social and religious life of African communities. The aesthetic appeal of music, while important, was of much less significance than in the Europe of the post-Middle Ages.

There are other differences. European music and song had long become formalised with its neatly-patterned structure as, for example, its division into regularly formed verses. This formalisation of European music does not mean that African music was crude. An investigation into Ashanti singing in 1817 revealed a highly sophisticated vocal tradition. This was less than a decade after the official ending of the slave trade to North America and clearly indicates that the music taken to America by slaves, while less rigidly structured than European music and with no written notation, was no less important, solidly established, and well-developed.

Certain vocal techniques in African music differ notably from the European tradition and they also had an important place in the development of Afro-American music. Singers do not necessarily begin a song by hitting a note squarely but slide up to it and similarly slide down from a note at the end of a song. In addition the bending of notes, the use of 'impure' notes, vocal buzzes and glottal sounds, are all elements which made for sharp differences between the song of Europe and Africa when the two met again (for they had met on many previous occasions in the past) on the American continent. That these differences are much less noticeable today is a mark of the great influence African musical tradition has had upon European ears. A typical example would be almost any concert performance by Ray Charles, at which can be heard all such elements, either singly or collectively.

In order to examine more closely the blending and assimilation which took place, some of the individual musical forms of the African in America should be considered. Among the earliest types of song permitted, even encouraged, by the white masters was the work song, a form of music-making well-established in African life.

The work song uses a call-and-response structure which became highly significant in the development of jazz. In America, the African work song was considered by white overseers to be of positive value, bringing as it did an impetus to the rigorous labours of the slaves. By tradition it included accented rhythms which could be adapted to synchronise with the need for sudden, concerted efforts, and words and harmonies were relatively unimportant. The voice was used more as an instrument than as a means of communication of information and ideas. The emotional content was unaffected, except when it was enhanced by such techniques as syncopations, alterations to pitch and innumerable vocal embellishments. Songs were thus varied according to the needs of the performance – a tradition of improvisation which considerably antedates jazz. Another form taken by the work song, and which also used a variation upon the call-and-response structure, was the field holler.

The solitary worker might also sing, but here there was no need for a coordinated structure. As a consequence, his singing could and did become more introspective and, in the words of Eileen Southern, 'his song took on the nature of a deeply personal utterance. Tempo, text, melody – all these things were manipulated by the worker to fit his mood of the moment.'

The content of some of these songs had many uses among which were the transmission of messages of hope from group to group, the singer's simple need to declare his or her existence, and a means of combating fatigue and despair.

White listeners put a different interpretation on such outpourings. Southern society was riddled with fear of uprising and revolt, and eventually the South became an armed camp. In such a climate of terror, singing in the fields was readily transmuted into aural evidence of the contentment of the singers. The myth of the contented darkie singing in the fields under the benign guardianship of the white master was thus born – and it took a long time to die.

The religious music of the slave was also subject to a great deal of mythmaking. The form and purpose of much religious music among slaves was highly complex and even today historians hold differing views of the true nature and importance of what became known as the 'negro spiritual'. For many whites in the South before the Civil

14

War, hearing their slaves singing hymns and songs based upon tales from the Bible was as reassuring as the singing in the fields. They readily convinced themselves that this was a sign of acceptance and passivity, and therefore those who sang spirituals were not to be feared. The new debate among historians has convinced many that those who sang this form of song drew from the Bible not so much the strength with which to bear the burden of slavery but rather found parallels with the oppression of other peoples, most notably the Jews under the Egyptians, and sought from the Scriptures hope of freedom in a new Promised Land.

The highly accessible form taken by both religious and entertainment music soon led to copying by white musicians and singers. It was changed, of course, and while change is not in itself bad there is little to commend the sentimentalisation of the music or the apparent need for white entertainers to black-up in order to deliver their 'compositions' with simulated authenticity. Plantation songs, coon songs, and the like became the stock-in-trade of tent show performers and the blackface minstrel was soon an integral part of white American culture.

Blackface entertainers were known towards the end of the eighteenth century but it was early in the next century that two basic stereotypes were formed in the minstrel shows and, in one guise or another, continued to appear on stage, on radio, in film and TV, for the next century and a half. These stereotypes were the bumbling, slow-moving, shuffling, countrified illiterate and his sharp, snappily-dressed, mildly larcenous citified cousin. The latter was personified as Zip Coon while the former was given a name which owed its origins to a song written by Thomas Dartmouth 'Daddy' Rice around 1818. Basing words, music and accompanying dance on something he had seen and heard performed by an elderly, crippled black groom, Rice's song helped him achieve fame as the nation's foremost blackface entertainer. The name in the title passed into the language and became the term used to describe discrimination and segregation – Jim Crow.

It was after the American Civil War that the most dramatic changes in the music of black Americans took place. The post-war years were not, of course, happy times for them. In many instances the infamous rules of conduct and repressive laws instigated throughout the South made life even harder than it had been under slavery, thus giving rise to the myth that blacks had been happier and better off under slavery than they were as freedmen. In many instances this was undoubtedly true. That this was a result of white oppression after the Civil War had been fought and lost somewhat diminishes the value of the argument. It was in the thirty-five years between the ending of hostilities and the end of the nineteenth century that the work song and, more particularly, the field holler began to develop into a more refined, more bitterly personal narrative ballad, peculiar to the descendants of former slaves. This would eventually become the blues. The cakewalk, the music of minstrelsy, and other forms of entertainment music were picked up by itinerant black musicians (who were following a tradition known in Africa) and the pianists among them developed a syncopated style of playing which eventually became formalised as ragtime. This music, already transmuted from earlier forms which were themselves amalgams of many traditions from other cultures, influenced, and were in turn influenced by, the music of many lands.

A useful focus of the blending of musical heritages from many parts of the world is New Orleans. This is not to view the city as the 'birthplace' of jazz, which is only one of innumerable oversimplifications in early histories of the music, but as it really was, a cosmopolitan microcosm. It was here, more than in any other single connurbation in North America, that most of the many strands which helped form the music that eventually became known as jazz, came together and fused into a single yet complex, and for a while still primitive, whole.

New Orleans was always a lively place and its music in these years matched every other aspect of its cultural life. The city's most renowned white composer, Louis Gottschalk (1829–69), worked in the established classical tradition, although he was influenced by the Spanish rhythms which he heard locally. All forms of black music could be heard too, from spirituals and hymn singing, narrative ballads and the ragtime piano players to the earlier forms from which these hybrids had sprung: the work song, the cakewalk and the camp song among them. But there was much more besides.

The white community in nineteenth century New Orleans was made up primarily of English-speaking native-born Americans,

French-speaking native-born Americans (known as Creoles), and relatively recent arrivals including Irish and Germans. In 1860, on the eve of the Civil War, the black community made up approximately one-seventh of the city's population and swelled rapidly after Emancipation in 1863.

Musicians in nineteenth-century New Orleans were both white and black, with *Créoles de couleur* being initially dominant over their darker-skinned fellows. These coloured Creoles were of mixed race and usually French-speaking. In time, the word Creole came to apply only to them. Generally speaking, they considered music an important part of their education and were trained in the classical European tradition. They played popular songs of the period, dance music and tunes from operettas and operas. New Orleans was the first American city to have a regular operatic season and its opera houses were sufficiently frequented by blacks to warrant special sections of seats reserved for freedmen and slaves.

Unlike the sophisticated coloured Creoles, the darker-skinned blacks were often musically illiterate and cruder in performance. Nevertheless, despite essential differences, when these two groups played music they drew largely from the same basic musical stock.

In the late-nineteenth century, as the city's wealth grew (it was the South's principal gateway for imports and exports) so too did demand for entertainment. With the 'anything goes' attitude displayed by the city's political bosses, sources of entertainment flourished. A city ordinance of 1898 set aside an area in which prostitution, while not legal, was not actively proscribed. This area was known as Storyville (after Sidney Story, the city alderman who proposed the legislation) and while the district's importance in the development of jazz has been massively overstated, its existence indicates official encouragement. Residents and visitors alike could expect, and find, a good time.

Eventually, this mixture of freedom and restriction – trained and self-taught musicians, light and dark-skinned negroes and whites, and the wide-open festive nature of much of the city – blended with existing and developing musical traditions to form a new kind of music which had a recognisable shape and character. That such a development occurred appears inevitable given the fluid nature of the music concentrated in the American South. That this new music should prove to be the only American art-form to gain international acceptance was remarkably fortuitous. Given that its origins lay in oppression – centuries of forcible servitude, and misery – its success is little short of astonishing. This new musical form was eventually given a name – jazz. And with jazz came the jazz singers – in all their myriad styles and forms.

2 The Empress, King Louis and Sweet Mama Stringbean

The use of folk melodies and ethnic musical forms by composers working in a more formalised manner is not, of course, something uniquely American. European composers have used folk music throughout the centuries. In nineteenth-century America, this use of traditional forms was adopted by composers as different as Louis Gottschalk from New Orleans, who was white with French and English ancestry; Stephen Foster, also white but northern-born and educated; and James A. Bland, who was born into a black middle-class family living in New York.

While Gottschalk worked almost entirely in the classical mould, albeit drawing heavily upon sometimes less-conventional sources for his inspiration, Foster (1826–64) became America's leading writer of popular songs. Much of his best-known, and longest-lasting output was couched in quasi-Negro form which heavily over-sentimentalised the music and condition of black Americans. Foster's enormous popularity lay in part in the fact that his career paralleled the rising tide of northern interest in, and concern for, the fate of slaves in the South. His songs, for which he earned practically nothing (he died an alcoholic pauper at the age of thirty-eight), evoked deep, if maudlin responses in American hearts. *Oh! Susannah, De Camptown Races, Swanee River, My Old Kentucky Home, Jeannie With the Light Brown Hair* and *Beautiful Dreamer* were just a handful of the sentimental songs which oozed from his pen.

Despite his comfortable beginnings, James Bland (1854–1911)

also ended his life in poverty after being the toast of New York and London (where he performed his songs for Queen Victoria). Bland's best-known songs, written very much in accordance with the minstrel show tradition of soulful ballads interspersed with lively, high-steppin' numbers, are *Carry Me Back To Old Virginny* and *Oh! Dem Golden Slippers*.

Regardless of race, musical value, source of inspiration and the like, the work of Foster and Bland carries with it only the faintest echoes of the music of Afro-Americans. Nevertheless, coming as they did, in the middle of the second half of the century, their songs helped prepare the American public for a new kind of music. While not essentially black, nor even folk music, their work had an air and suggested ideas that had hitherto been alien to the musical establishment.

Foster and Bland in the field of popular music, and Gottschalk in the classical form, absorbed much that was black but their diluted output carried Afro-American musical forms no further. Fortunately, however, there were numerous fine composers who were also drawing upon the same basic sources but whose talents and inclinations caused them to develop in a very different manner. The best-known and most influential of his time was Scott Joplin (1868–1917) whose use of folk music, dance tunes and ballads similarly took heed of those 'alien' forms but he became one of a huge band of performers and composers who transformed American popular music in the late-nineteenth century with the introduction of ragtime.

Joplin was born in Texas and while still a very young teenager earned a living playing piano in his home state and in Louisiana. He settled eventually in St Louis, a city which, with nearby Sedalia, soon became a major centre of ragtime music. Joplin's compositions include *The Entertainer*, the exquisite *Solace* (both of which became enormously popular many years later, thanks to their use on the soundtrack of the 1973 film *The Sting*), *Elite Syncopations*, *Pineapple Rag* and his most successful tune, *Maple Leaf Rag*.

The essential ingredient of ragtime is its highly developed use of syncopation. Syncopated rhythm can be defined as a musical device wherein the pianist uses his right (treble) hand to place accents on the normally unaccented second and third beats of a measure while maintaining a regular accented beat with the left (bass) hand. While not uncommon in European music, this effect was used only sparingly and then for short periods of time. In ragtime, the device is used continually and hence builds up a driving, rhythmic propulsion hitherto unknown to formally-schooled musicians. For their harmonies, ragtime composers drew heavily upon contemporary popular music, especially such devices as the 'banjo chords' and attempted imitation of brass band music then popularised by John Philip Sousa.

Although essentially music for the piano, ragtime had an associated vocal tradition from its earliest stirrings. In the minstrel shows the coon-song singers and comedy dancers adopted ragtime and a national craze developed, aided greatly by the introduction of piano-roll players and early phonographs. The complexities inherent in scoring ragtime were not fully resolved until as late as 1897 with the publication of Tom Turpin's *Harlem Rag* (following closely on the heels of W.H. Krell's *Mississippi Rag* which was the first rag to be copyrighted). The craze, the accessibility of this new musical form, and the fact that it could now be written down, led to every songwriting hack in the nation turning his hand to so-called rags. Additionally, thanks to a flood of sheet music, everyone with a piano could attempt to perform the music of black Americans in front parlours across the country and, of course, everyone could sing – however badly.

In one sense, that of the long-term benefits to popular music, it did not matter that much of the material so published, played and sung owed precious little to the Afro-American origins of the genuine article, or that the bulk of the new rags fell short of the quality of those written by Joplin and his peers, or that black-faced white minstrels were still poking vicious fun at blacks through their caricatured Jim Crows and Zip Coons. For all its flaws and shortcomings, this was the beginning of acceptance for black music in America. In the forefront of this new popularity came a number of composers, singers, and other performers whose influences echo through the years. Among them were artists who brought real black faces to the stages of Broadway even if, in many instances, they had to be applied with just as much burnt cork as their white counterparts.

ck faces had to be artificially blackened in order to
e pretext that these artists were not really black at all, so
ne-century Broadway shows had to be essentially European
structure and tradition even if black artists were performing in
them. Many were orthodox operettas which gave only a passing nod
towards America and Americans. One of the leading singers of the
day, Sissieretta Jones, was even billed as 'the Black Patti', thus
deferring to the famous operatic singer Adelina Patti.

The bending of the emerging music to suit white tastes and
sensibilities was not the province of the lower, working classes (into
which could be lumped the vast majority of black Americans in the
half-century following the end of the Civil War). Like Bland before
them, the most successful black composers of the period, James
Weldon Johnson, Bob Cole and J. Rosamond Johnson, were all
middle-class. These composers readily adapted the music of their
fellows in such a manner that it found immediate acceptance among
white audiences.

Vaudeville performer Ben Harney (1871–1938) took this adaptation
to even greater extremes than most of his contemporaries. For
many years he was thought to have been a white man but pianist-
composer Eubie Blake, in conversation with Alec Wilder, stated that
Harney was black, passing for white. (Blake went on to praise
Harney as the true father of stride piano, thus predating James P.
Johnson by several years.) Certainly, Harney sang and played very
much in the true tradition of black Americans. Although subjected
to some modification, his best-known composition, *You've Been A
Good Old Wagon But You've Done Broke Down*, was performed
regularly through the 1930s and can still be heard today. Harney's
claims to have been the sole inventor of ragtime were clearly inflated,
yet if Blake is right about his piano-playing then he is certainly more
important than has been hitherto acknowledged.

Of all the black entertainers to gain acceptance on white stages,
Bert Williams (c.1876–1922) was the best-known and best-loved
although it must be doubted if New York audiences ever fully
understood the subtleties of his performances. His on-stage persona,
that of a hapless individual beaten down by life, carried with it much
more of the reality of the black experience in America than the
surface image of yet another coon caricature suggested. Williams had

22

been one half of the Walker and Williams vaudeville team but his partner's ill-health and early death thrust him on alone and he became a leading performer with the Ziegfield Follies, the apogee of 1920s theatreland. Williams' classic performance was of a tune to which he spoke, rather than sang, the lyric. *Nobody* became so much a part of the real man and the character he portrayed that with his death the song fell into disuse. Its revival in the late-1970s by Ben Vereen, a talented entertainer, missed the point of its origins, settling instead for banal sentimentality in place of Williams' moving depiction of the real life of many black Americans.

Several of the most influential black American songwriters and performers died in the early years of the twentieth century. Bob Cole, George Walker and Ernest Hogan (a popular artist on the vaudeville circuit, who wrote the unfortunately titled *All Coons Look Alike To Me*) all died in 1909, thus weakening the grip black music was beginning to exert. With the passage of time, the conscience of white America, pricked by awareness of the treatment of blacks during the aftermath of the Civil War, had been eased. The depression of 1893 had damaged interracial feelings as whites and blacks competed for too few jobs. These feelings were exacerbated by urban unrest, including the Jack Johnson riots following the boxing match in which the black heavyweight demolished James J. Jeffries. The deaths of leading black artists, coinciding as they did with an increase in racial tension, prompted a decline in the acceptability of blacks in white theatreland. Soon, blacks had all but vanished from the sight of white audiences, with only Bert Williams retaining his prominence. Blacks continued performing, of course, but were now reduced to the minor vaudeville circuits and those, like the Theatre Owners' Booking Association (known as Tobytime to the performers – or Tough on Black Asses to those who were dissatisfied with their deal), which catered exclusively for audiences on the black theatre circuit.

The extension of ragtime singing which found favour with white Broadway audiences, aligned as it was with the European traditions of operetta and ballad-singing, was the more sophisticated of two broad bands of song finding popularity at the time. The second band, while also developing through the minstrel show, stayed much closer to other, earthier traditions. This form of ragtime vocalising found an astonishingly varied mixture of performers, only some of whom worked in the emergent jazz idiom. Among them were Tony Jackson, Jelly Roll Morton, Sophie Tucker, Al Jolson, Nora Bayes and Fanny Brice.

If Jelly Roll Morton is to be believed, the black pianist and singer Tony Jackson (1876–1921) was deservedly termed 'The world's greatest single-handed entertainer'. Given that Morton seldom said anything very complimentary about anyone other than himself, Jackson must have been quite an artist. A pianist, who enjoyed playing all musical forms from the orthodox European classics to the rags of his own era, Jackson also sang in what has been described as an extraordinarily wide vocal range. Wherever he played, Jackson attracted enormous attention, especially after he had left his native New Orleans to take up residence in Chicago in 1905 where he remained until his death. Although he composed many songs, Jackson preferred working as an entertainer. He considered selling songs for a few dollars each to be hardly worth the effort, a comment which reflects more upon the suspect nature of the music publishing business of his time than upon the man himself. A tiny handful of Jackson's songs were published and of these only *Pretty Baby* has lived on to the present day.

As for Ferdinand 'Jelly Roll' Morton (1885–1941), he, more than any other jazz musician of any era, has suffered a form of character assassination unwittingly brought upon himself. Morton was born of mixed racial ancestry and became a leading exponent of the developing musical forms of his native New Orleans. His aggressive self-promotion claimed, among other things, astonishing sexual prowess (hence his nickname) and the fact that he had, single-handedly, created jazz. At one time or another he also laid claim to inventing the blues, and might well have claimed ragtime as his own too if Ben Harney had not beaten him to that particular boast. If Morton had defined more sharply his claim – to that of creating jazz piano – he might have found it easier to substantiate. Unfortunately for his reputation, his extravagant claims irritated musicians in the 1930s. When they rightly debunked his hyperbole they also unfairly dumped his genuine achievements so effectively that even today, long after his death, his true status is seldom adequately appraised.

Morton was a fine pianist, adept at ragtime and jazz, an effective if limited singer, a highly skilled arranger whose work foreshadowed that of later, better-known men, and a composer of great talent. His songs include *Mr Jelly Lord*, *Sweet Substitute* and *I'm Alabama Bound*. Morton's singing voice was of limited range but was highly expressive, witness the self-mocking *joie de vivre* of his declamatory vocal chorus in *Doctor Jazz*. His recordings of 1940 and 1941 evidence a ragtime-cum-blues style of vocalising of a past era – a time when Ben Harney was causing a stir in New York and entertainers of similar persuasion were to be heard on the vaudeville circuits and in red-light districts throughout the land. Yet there is tenderness too, as on *Mamie's Blues* when Morton recalls Mamie Desdoumes and reflectively sings of times long past. His vocals on *Buddy Bolden's Blues*, *Sweet Substitute*, *Michigan Water Blues* and *Don't You Leave Me Here* are all evocative of those times and are sung and played with a simple but moving depth of feeling. Conversely, Morton's wry asides on *Big Lip Blues* and *My Home Is In A Southern Town* are worthy of a present-day cabaret singer while the vaudeville overtones of *Good Old New York*, recorded in 1940, barely hint at the hard times he was then enduring.

Despite Morton's fanciful claims to have invented jazz, no one would dispute his being a jazz performer, while it may be difficult for today's audiences to associate Sophie Tucker, Al Jolson and other contemporary white vaudevilleans within the same context. Quite clearly, they are not jazz singers but they contributed to the growing climate of acceptance wherein true jazz singing was allowed freer rein. Through use of syncopated rhythms and by popularisation of songs with musical origins in ragtime and the blues, they helped prepare the way for what was to come.

Sophie Tucker (1884–1966) was born in Russia and is remembered as 'the last of the Red Hot Mommas', a phrase taken from a song written especially for her after she had gained national fame. In her early career, which began in 1906 when she won an amateur talent contest in New York, Sophie appeared in blackface. In her case blackface was not merely a theatrical convention, it was also a psychological defence because she was a big woman who believed herself to be physically unattractive. The accidental loss of her make-up forced her on-stage one night without this defence but her powerful personality so overwhelmed her audience that she never blacked-up again. Sophie drew her repertoire from all available sources: she sang rags (*That Lovin' Rag* and *The Darktown Strutters Ball*) and would happily take new material by comparative unknowns and apply her unmistakable personal stamp. One such song, brought to her by Shelton Brooks, a talented entertainer in the Bert Williams tradition, she liked from the moment it was first demonstrated to her. She sang it for the rest of her long career and *Some Of These Days* became not just the hallmark of a Sophie Tucker performance but forever afterwards imparted an aural image of an era. Sophie's singing voice was not best suited for the performance of the blues although she gained from listening to blues singers, such as Ethel Waters and Alberta Hunter but, as Hunter was later to admit, the influence was by no means one-way. In her performances, Sophie could demonstrate a conviction lacking in many of the singers who came to prominence during the blues revival of the 1940s and 1950s. For the jazz listener, however, the content of her repertoire was overburdened with songs that were maudlin in both content and performance.

A contemporary of Sophie Tucker, Al Jolson (1886–1950) was also born in Russia. After leaving his orthodox religious background (his father was a synagogue cantor) he worked with various minstrel shows, which included the most famous in the land, until he emerged as a solo act of astonishing power and durability. Jolson drew inspiration from fellow minstrel acts and from ragtime (among his hit songs was Tony Jackson's *Pretty Baby*). Although he never progressed further than an amalgam of such music together with operetta, his vocal inflections and syncopated phrasing influenced many younger and decidedly diverse singers, including Ethel Waters, Bing Crosby and Connee Boswell, who in their turn would directly influence innumerable other singers.

Nora Bayes and Fanny Brice also brought elements of ethnic music to a wider audience. Both began their careers as 'coon-shouters' in smalltime vaudeville but made it to the very top, which for all such entertainers meant Broadway in the Ziegfield Follies. Bayes popularised all manner of songs including *Take Me Out To The Ball Game*, *I'll Be With You In Apple Blossom Time*, *Over There* and *Shine On Harvest Moon*. Brice's repertoire was similarly a mixture of comic songs, ragtime novelties and sentimental ballads, which in her case carried an element of pathos imparted by her plain-featured gawkiness. Songs like *Second Hand Rose* and *My Man* lived on long after her death and earned a revival thanks to Barbra Streisand's renditions in her screen portrayal of Fanny in *Funny Girl* (1964).

Popular as these white artists were, they were all a far cry from the genuinely black musical tradition of ragtime from which they drew so much. They were even further from another black musical form which grew alongside ragtime and which eventually touched every facet of American popular song of the twentieth century. This was the blues.

The blues is a musical form which can be considered in a variety of ways, among these are the poetic and the technical for, as Paul Oliver has observed, 'the blues is both a state of mind and a music which gives voice to it'. Technically, the blues is frequently (but not exclusively) a twelve-bar chord sequence in which the third and seventh notes are bent. Poetically, the blues can evoke all of human experience. Thus, while an instrumentalist might say, 'I'm going to play *a* blues', a singer may well express it differently: 'I'm going to sing *the* blues'. What a blues is not, as Alberta Hunter commented, is a sad song sung slow. The blues can be sad, and the blues can be sung slow, but the blues can also be happy and fast, an evocation of spiritual needs or of earthy desires. It can, and often is, about lost love but it can also amuse or inform, proselytise or preach, anger or entertain. Often it can accomplish more than one of these functions at the same time. The blues can be a public celebration or condemnation, or it can be a highly personal account of deeply-felt private emotion. It can be rural or urban, it can be art or it can be commercially exploitative. Indeed, it can be almost anything its practitioner wants it to be.

The blues is thus so diverse that isolating a point in time when it becomes identifiable is clearly impossible. Ma Rainey, one of the earliest 'classic' blues singers, was bold enough to put a date on her first recognition of the form. 1902 might well have also been the 'birth-date' but, then again, so too might almost any other year around the turn of the century.

Of undoubted and important assistance in the rapid popularisation of the blues, and in helping it to change the face of all American popular music, was the development of the phonograph. After Thomas A. Edison's invention in 1877 little happened for a decade as the novelty's potential was not recognised. Serious manufacturing of phonographs was begun in 1888 by Edison's North American Phonograph Company. This company failed but one of its regional subsidiaries, Columbia, prospered and was soon a serious competitor for Edison's new firm, the National Phonographic Company. Another competitor, National Gramophone, led the change from cylinders to discs around 1897, and from 1902 onwards Columbia too turned to discs. In 1901 National Gramophone became the Victor Talking Machine Company and the following year issued six sides by the Dinwiddie Coloured Quartet, reputedly the first recordings to offer authentic American Negro music. Described in the company's catalogue as genuine jubilee and camp meeting shouts, the Dinwiddie Quartet's songs included *Steal Away*, *My Way Is Cloudy* and *Gabriel's Trumpet*.

This instance apart, black artists were largely ignored during the early years of the record industry. The Chicago *Defender*, one of the nation's two leading black newspapers, campaigned unsuccessfully against this slight and it was not until three years after the 1917 recordings by the white Original Dixieland Jazz Band that black artists began serious recording of authentic black music.

The importance of the role of records in the development of American popular music cannot be overstressed. Not only did records allow a far wider public to hear the work of artists they might never be able to hear in person, but records were also heard by other singers and, more importantly, by the children who would become the next generation of singers. They grew up with the music and voices of established songwriters and singers in their ears although, of course, many of the singers they heard were neither jazz singers nor were influenced by jazz. Indeed, given the nature of the record industry, then as now, many were inept in any genre. Nevertheless, cross-fertilisation of ideas and styles was non-stop. As Leroy Ostransky has observed, for the 'seminal jazz figures in all cities, records were the stuff that shaped and moulded their tastes, technique, and ultimately their very lives'.

The first singer to record the blues was Mamie Smith who gained the opportunity almost by accident. Two popular songs written by

Perry Bradford were to have been recorded by Sophie Tucker but contractual problems prevented her from making the date. Bradford persuaded the record company boss, Fred Hager, to try Mamie Smith, an unknown young black woman. Hager took the chance, the records were reasonably successful and later that same year, on 20 August 1920, Mamie Smith entered the OKeh studios once more and this time recorded *Crazy Blues*. Sales of more than 100,000 copies were enough to prompt the launch of numerous other artists, of decidedly variable quality, on careers as blues singers. Most important of all, the blues was established as a viable form of music in an industry geared to commercial success and the consequent spread and development of this musical form was thus ensured.

Mamie Smith (1883–1946) has been underrated for too long. Although not in the majestic class of Bessie Smith or Ma Rainey, and not possessing the subtleties of Ethel Waters, she had a vigorous delivery and considerable stage presence. A volatile performer, Mamie could hold an audience with her buoyant interpretation of the blues and related material.

Her *Crazy Blues* may sound a little wooden today, mainly due to the accompanying band, but later recordings offer far better examples of her direct style. *Goin' Crazy With The Blues*, recorded in 1926, shows Mamie at her mature best as she drives the melody along with good support from Tom Morris (cnt) and Charlie Irvis (tb). Good examples of her syncopated style are to be heard on such titles as *Jenny's Ball* and *What Have You Done To Make Me Feel This Way*.

Although Mamie Smith may go down as the first singer to record the blues, she was much more a vaudeville artist than a blues singer. It seems probable that Lucille Hegamin (1894–1970) was the first true blues singer to record. She quickly followed Mamie into the studios and in November 1920 recorded *The Jazz Me Blues* and *Everybody's Blues*. She was a clear-voiced singer with a wide repertoire and sang with good blues feeling. She will always be associated with Lemuel Fowler's composition *He May Be Your Man*

But He Comes To See Me Sometimes, which she recorded on a number of occasions.

In New York in 1922, at a grand concert and dance attended by the State Governor and Fiorello H. La Guardia, the future mayor, the feature of the evening was a blues contest. Lucille Hegamin competed with Trixie Smith, Daisy Martin and Alice Carter. After singing for an hour, Trixie Smith was declared the winner with Lucille Hegamin a close second.

Trixie Smith (1895–1943) was a light-voiced artist of limited power and range. Nevertheless, she recorded some fine performances. *The Railroad Blues*, recorded in 1925, with Louis Armstrong (tp) and Charlie Green (tb) accompanying her superbly, is perhaps the finest example of Trixie's cabaret style. Another stomping performance is heard on *The World's Jazz Crazy Lawdy So Am I* which aptly captures the mood of the lyrics. In the jazz and blues revival of the late 1930s she recorded *Freight Train Blues* and, while there seems to be little commitment on her part, the band, which includes Sidney Bechet (cl), sets the performance alight. In her last recording, in 1939, on which she is accompanied by Henry 'Red' Allen (tp), she sings *No Good Man* with rather more feeling.

Among other singers of the day was Edith Wilson (1896–1981), an extremely fine vaudevillean who recorded many superb performances which unfortunately suffer from poor recording techniques. *What Do You Care*, with excellent cornet breaks by Johnny Dunn, is among her finest recordings. She had the widest repertoire of all the early performers, moving from risqué blues to slapstick comedy in her cabaret act. Her recording of *Rules And Regulations Signed Razor Jim* is full of humour and, surprisingly for 1922, she conveys considerable swing. Similarly good-humoured is *He May Be Your Man But He Comes To See Me Sometimes*, also with Johnny Dunn.

Rosa Henderson is another fine example of the early vaudeville blues artist. She was accompanied by some of the finest contemporary jazz musicians and featured typical vaudeville numbers of the day. Her recordings included good performances of *Get It Fixed*, recorded in 1925, and *Can't Be Bothered With No Sheik* in 1931.

In the course of the few years after Mamie Smith's groundbreaking recording the use of blues singers boomed and they were soon heard by a far wider audience than could ever hear them in theatres or travelling shows. Although the problem of colour was theoretically overcome (on records there was no need for segregation of audiences, blacking-up, or any of the other devices associated with live performances), the record companies maintained division by establishing what were known as 'coloured catalogues', a term soon abandoned in favour of 'race records'. The term 'race' was much in use in black middle-class communities as part of a conscious attempt to consolidate their small gains as they ascended laboriously through American society. Few of the record companies were owned by blacks, however, and the financial reins were thus controlled, as always, by white entrepreneurs and businessmen. Race records, at least initially, were bought largely by blacks and this market proved unexpectedly profitable. Certainly, it was enough to rescue some companies from bankruptcy.

Although she did not record until 1923, Ma Rainey (1886–1939) was in a completely different class to most of the singers previously discussed. Born in Georgia, she married Will Rainey when she was eighteen and accompanied him in travelling shows. Billed as 'Rainey and Rainey – The Assassinators of the Blues', they worked together for a number of years. Rainey and Rainey were typical of the tent show acts, featuring comedy and dancing as well as singing. From the moment she first heard 'them blues' in 1902, Ma Rainey featured such songs as a finale to her act, thus becoming one of the first artists to perform the blues on stage. In later years, after the break-up of her marriage to Will Rainey, her use of the blues gradually increased. She became known as 'The Mother of the Blues' and hers were earthy blues, harsh and direct in their content, and when she too recorded she brought into the studios none of the vaudevillean glossiness of those lesser singers who had preceded her.

Her Paramount recordings, though of poor technical quality, show Ma Rainey to have a sombre majesty and strength of delivery which few other blues singers have ever matched. *Jelly Bean Blues*, *Counting The Blues* and the superb *See See Rider*, with sensitive cornet accompaniment by a very young Louis Armstrong with a Fletcher Henderson group, are among the finest examples of her dignified approach to the blues. The same qualities can be heard on *Southern Blues*, *Bo-Weavil Blues* and *Cell Bound Blues*, with trumpet by Tommy Ladnier. Ma Rainey's tent show background is well in

31

Ma Rainey – sombre majesty; (*left to right*) Alberta Hunter – astonishing control; Ethel Waters – emotionally dramatic; Ida Cox – threatening.

evidence on *Ma Rainey's Black Bottom*, which she sings with considerable humour, as indeed she does the last two songs she ever recorded (in 1928) with Papa Charlie Jackson: *Big Feeling Blues* and *Ma And Pa's Poorhouse Blues*, but by this time, her downhome delivery was out of favour.

A tough, rumbustious woman, Ma Rainey collected about her a variety of tales which concerned themselves with her unusual and wide-ranging sexual appetites and proclivities, and of her fearsomeness when crossed. As always happens in such cases, her abilities as a singer were thus shadowed by matters of little consequence. Sadly, although she lived well into the era of sound movies, she was never filmed in performance. Given the recollections of those who did see her, Ma Rainey on stage must have been an extraordinary experience, although perhaps not always as intended. New Orleans drummer Zutty Singleton recalled her singing in his home town with the travelling tent show. In one song, as she came to the words: 'look what a hole I'm in' – the stage collapsed.

Ma Rainey influenced most of the blues singers of her own generation and was a prime influence in the careers of the singers who followed her. Among them was a young woman named Bessie Smith who came from Chattanooga, Tennessee.

Bessie Smith (c.1894–1937) made her professional debut at the tender age of nine. She quickly toughened up. Bessie was a complex, aggressive individual, not averse to violence when she thought the need arose or when she was drinking, and by all accounts one or the other of these two prompts was usually in force. But, as a singer of the blues she was supreme. In Bessie's performances can be heard the crystallisation of the classic blues form. It is a curious combination of folk and vaudeville traditions, performed with a subtle jazz inflection and the deepest and most searing of feelings. Her genius is revealed not only in her grand theatrical manner, nor even simply in her rich, contralto voice. It is the combination of these effects allied to her heartfelt emotions and an innate rhythmic and soaring swing, which makes each soulful interpretation a stirring jazz performance. The white writer and socialite Carl Van Vechten had this to say of her: 'This was no actress; no imitator of woman's woes; there was no pretence. It was the real thing; a woman cutting her heart open with a knife until it was exposed for us all to see, so that we suffered as she suffered, exposed with a rhythmic ferocity which could hardly be borne.'

In everything Bessie sang, be it a slow blues or an uproarious tale of loose living, there was in her voice an ever-present undertone of tragedy. It is unlikely that Bessie was ever formally taught by Ma Rainey (although their paths did occasionally cross and for a time they worked together in a tent show) but it is obvious that she learned much from listening to the older woman. Some of Bessie's earliest recordings show clear signs of Rainey's influence, in particular *Bo-Weavil Blues* and *Moonshine Blues* which are replete with folk imagery. Bessie herself, however, acknowledged the influence of an obscure, now-forgotten blues singer named Cora Fisher.

There are many highlights in Bessie's recording career, and none is more impressive than her collaboration with Louis Armstrong for Columbia. Armstrong's inspired cornet obbligatos perfectly underline the awesome voice on their justly famous recordings. *Careless Love* is a fine example; then there is *J.C. Holmes Blues* on which Charlie Green's trombone joins Armstrong to bolster superbly Bessie's uncompromising vocal. The superlative voice and the cornet accompaniment are undeterred by Fred Longshaw's harmonium on *St Louis Blues* and the heartfelt cry of *Reckless Blues* is a truly great interpetation:

I ain't good looking but I'm somebody's angel child.

To listen to the Bessie and Louis recordings in their entirety is to glory in great music almost too richly beautiful to absorb. They are among the major achievements of the classic blues era; yet they are not alone in their magnificence. The soulful cornet of Joe Smith may not have measured up to the gigantic talent of Armstrong but his firm and sophisticated accompaniment, more subservient than Armstrong's, suited Bessie admirably. She appears to have preferred working with Joe, who proved ideal for the more light-hearted numbers such as *Cakewalkin' Babies, Alexander's Ragtime Band* and the lusty swing of *There'll Be A Hot Time In The Old Town Tonight*. His playing on *Young Woman's Blues* is perhaps a little too lightweight but Bessie amply makes up for any deficiency with her vivid portrayal. Much the same can be said of *Send Me To The Electric Chair, Them's Graveyard Words* and *Hot Springs Blues*, where the

Bessie Smith – tragic undertones.

concentrated bitterness of her attack is enough to seize and hold the attention.

Another collaboration which must rank with Bessie's finest comes on her recordings with trumpet player Tommy Ladnier. He accompanies her with great authority on *Dyin' By The Hour*, which Bessie sings with sober resignation, and on *Foolish Man Blues*. But, so many of her performances are classic: *Sweet Mistreater*, *Lock and Key*, *Black Mountain Blues* with pianist James P. Johnson; *I've Got What It Takes But It Breaks My Heart To Give It Away* with cornetist Ed Allen; the intensely sombre *Nobody Knows You When You're Down And Out* are all sung with her tremendous sense of swing and delivered in that beautiful and imposing voice.

Audiences loved and idolised Bessie. Her live performances were said to be mesmeric experiences; but her years of great success were short lived. By the late 1920s the blues audience was changing. Now they wanted their blues more sophisticated, more in tune with the Roaring Twenties image. The influence of such white torch singers as Ruth Etting, Helen Morgan and Annette Hanshaw was felt even in the blues world. Bessie's tragic blues, with all their misery and grief, were no longer acceptable. In a 1928 Columbia recording session Bessie sang a touchingly autobiographical *Me And My Gin* wherein she concludes:

> When I'm feeling high
> Ain't nothin' I want to do (×2)
> Keep me full of gin
> And I'd sure be nice to you.

But, singers like Ethel Waters were in the ascendancy and in 1931 Bessie was dropped by Columbia.

Unreliable and no longer popular with Harlem night people, she was obliged to resort once more to touring the South. In 1933, John Hammond brought Bessie back to the recording studios for what proved to be her final session. Hammond, the son of a wealthy socialite family, was able to indulge his passion for music in general and jazz in particular. Fortunately, he did so with acumen, good taste, and a marvellous ear for new, or in this case, unused talent. Bessie was accompanied on this date by the superb Frankie Newton (tp),

Jack Teagarden (tb), Benny Goodman (cl) and Chu Berry (ts). *Gimme A Pigfoot* is a masterpiece, as is a commanding *Do Your Duty*. Still possessing wonderful control, she projects gloriously and is as strongly confident as ever.

Although Bessie died following a car crash in 1937, her influence echoes through the years and can be heard in such diverse performers as Billie Holiday, Mahalia Jackson, Dinah Washington and Aretha Franklin. She was, and remains, truly the Empress of the Blues.

Of the major blues singers only Clara Smith (1896–1935) can be closely compared to the great Bessie. (All the Smiths discussed here were unrelated.) Like Bessie, she was already playing to capacity crowds on the TOBA circuit when the 1920s recording boom occurred. Billed as 'The Queen of the Moaners', Clara specialised in slow, dragging blues which she sang in a drawling, lowdown manner. No other singer could display such poignancy at the extremely slow pace which Clara used with power and authority. It was this exceptionally slow delivery that made her performances so comparable to Bessie's. One outstanding example is her recording of *Whip It To A Jelly* which the listener expects to be taken at a jaunty tempo. Instead, Clara sings with slow, sensual relish:

> I wear my skirts up my knee
> And whip my jelly with who I please.

Her dirge-like interpretation produces a masterpiece; it is the definitive performance of the song. Surprisingly, Clara Smith was able to entertain both country audiences and Harlem sophisticates alike. The vaudeville side of her nature is best heard on humorous songs like *My Brand New Papa:*

> Hard to get, hard to please
> Got more lovin' than a dog has fleas.

Her *Salty Dog* is far superior in quality to the better-known version recorded by Papa Charlie Jackson and Freddie Keppard. Her duets with Bessie Smith, although successful, demonstrate the differences between the supreme Bessie and the slightly less authoritative Clara. Nevertheless, only Clara could possibly have engaged in a duet with the Empress and emerge unscathed and with reputation intact. Clara is at her resonant and melancholy best on *Sobbin' Sister Blues* and *Steamboat Stomp*, accompanied by Freddie Jenkins on trumpet.

All the great blues queens of the 1920s had a suitably regal quality about their work. Among the finest was Ida Cox (1900–67) who was born in Chattanooga, Tennessee. She ran away with a Southern minstrel show when she was fourteen and in her early travels performed with Jelly Roll Morton in Atlanta, then at Chicago's Plantation Club with King Oliver. Like her contemporary, Mamie Smith, Ida Cox enjoyed an aggressively opulent lifestyle – until the money ran out. For Ida, the money lasted longer than with most but this did not deter her from singing with conviction and sincerity such lines as:

I ain't got no money and my credit don't go no more.

Ida Cox recorded numerous titles for Paramount, many of them with Lovie Austin and her Blues Serenaders featuring the intense trumpet of Tommy Ladnier which perfectly complemented her singing. Ida delivered her blues and vaudeville songs in the same brooding monotone. Limiting as this was, she developed the continuous, almost threatening drone in her voice thus creating an altogether oppressive atmosphere. The implicit threat which she exudes in her often cynical performances is very evident in *Death Letter Blues* and *I've Got The Blues For Rampart Street*, with exceptional accompaniment from Ladnier and Jimmy Bryant (cl). The absurdity of this austere performer singing the somewhat ridiculous *Mama Doo Shee Blues* makes a surprisingly successful record. Her intense performance on *Bone Orchard Blues*, *Tree Top Tall Blues* and *Worn Down Daddy* reveals her at her greatest.

After several years in retirement, she returned to the studios in 1939 and recorded some excellent titles with an all-star group including Hot Lips Page (tp), Edmond Hall (cl) and Charlie Christian (g). Although past her peak, she retains much of the cynicism of her earlier work. *Hard Time Blues*, *Take Him Off My Mind*, *Pink Slip Blues* and *Deep Sea Blues* are particularly satisfying.

37

In 1940 she recorded excellent versions of *Last Mile Blues* and *I Can't Quit That Man* with Henry Allen (tp) and J.C. Higginbotham (tb). Her final appearance in the studios was in 1961 and, while these performances were less than wholly successful, she was still recognisably Ida Cox, 'The Blues Queen'.

If the blues of Ida Cox were oppressive, Victoria Spivey's blues were stark and sinister, dealing as they did with sickness, sadism, suicide and murder. Although her voice was neither rich nor deep, her acidic delivery with its menacing hint of savagery hold the listener's attention.

Many of the lurid blues Spivey (1906–76) sang were of her own creation and are notable for the originality of the lyrics. There are few traditional lines in a Spivey blues and there is a fascination about her barbarous imagery, as in *Blood Thirsty Blues:*

> Blood, blood, look at all that blood (×2)
> Yes I killed my man, a lowdown good for nothing cub
> I told him blood was in my eyes and still he
>   wouldn't listen to me (×2)
> Yes instead of giving him sugar, I put glass in his tea.

Equally fascinating is her casual reasoning when, after telling how she had poisoned her man, she sings:

> I done it in a passion
> I thought it was the fashion.

Few classic blues singers could have adequately coped with lyrics such as those in her *Moanin' The Blues* which has the astonishingly long line: 'I'm the only one in my family to take a biscuit to pieces and put it back just like it was'. Victoria Spivey not only copes with it but manages to sing the line with natural ease. A polished, extrovert performer, she was totally convincing on blues and jazz tunes alike as shown by her rousing tear-up on *Funny Feathers* and *How Do You Do It That Way* with a band led by Louis Armstrong. For a time she led Lloyd Hunter's Serenaders, a territory band, but some of her finest performances were in the company of blues singer and guitarist Lonnie Johnson, with *Dope Head Blues* and *Garter*

Snake Blues being typically bloodthirsty in content:

Because ooh, he's innocent as a garter snake (×2)
When I find the woman who stole him, her neck I mean to break.

Spivey was rediscovered in the 1960s blues boom and enjoyed the benefits of this resurgence until her death.

Sippie Wallace (1898–) made many distinguished recordings. A product of a large church-going family, she began performing professionally in tent shows where she acted and sang ballads. It was not until she recorded for OKeh that she began to sing the blues. Among the many top jazz artists who accompanied her were Sidney Bechet and Louis Armstrong. Of particular interest are her versions of *Special Delivery Blues*, *Jack Of Diamonds Blues* and *The Flood Blues*, all featuring excellent obbligatos by Armstrong. A tune with which Sippie Wallace will always be associated is *I'm A Mighty Tight Woman* which she recorded on several occasions. The definitive performance is that from 1929 with inspired accompaniment by the great New Orleans clarinetist, Johnny Dodds, who stimulates Sippie to heights she had not previously attained – and never would again. Her beautifully soaring vocal over Dodds' sensitive accompaniment transforms the number into a classic performance. Amazingly, Sippie Wallace proved a sensation at the 1982 Nice Jazz Festival, as much for her startling hats as for her singing, although that too was remarkably impressive. Helped onto the stage she looked, in her huge Merry Widow hat and voluminous dress, like a relic from a bygone age, but when she began to sing the years slipped easily away.

Born in Charleston, South Carolina, Bertha 'Chippie' Hill (1905–50) was a product of a large family. She began her singing career in Leroy's, the noted Harlem nightspot but later moved to Chicago. There she sang in dance halls where she was accompanied by many bands including King Oliver's. She made a number of superior recordings for OKeh, among the best being *Pratt City Blues* and *Kid Man Blues* on which she sings in the sombre straightforward tradition of Ma Rainey. Accompanying her, she has Louis Armstrong and pianist Richard M. Jones. After many years out of show business, Chippie Hill resurfaced in the 1940s. Much of her time was then spent singing at Jimmy Ryan's in New York where she would circle the floor singing a chorus at each table in the manner of the blues singers of old. Although still a vigorous performer her pitch was now uncertain. A well-loved artist, she was killed in a hit-and-run accident.

Among the countless vaudeville blues singers, the majority of whom were of uneven quality, were several fine artists who created an occasional miniature classic.

Lizzie Miles, who often sang in Louisiana Creole patois, worked with King Oliver in her early years. The Dixieland revival found her in roaring and robust form on the old popular tunes on which she was accompanied by various bands, including those of Sharkey Bonano and Bob Scobey. The Texas Moaner, Lillian Glinn, had a full voice and built a substantial if parochial reputation centred on her home town of Dallas. A most underrated performer, her classic recordings include *Shake 'Em Down* and *Atlanta Blues*. Mattie Hite sang with warmth and feeling; Laura Smith had a full, rounded voice and can be heard to good effect on *Don't You Leave Me*; Maggie Jones was superb on *Good Time Flat Blues* with Armstrong; Cleo Gibson recorded only two titles, one of which was the excellent and erotic *I've Got Ford Engine Movements In My Hips* on which she is backed by the searing trumpet of Henry Mason; Martha Copeland had the misfortune to be tagged 'Everybody's Mammy', which detracted from her distinctive style. Sara Martin added to her singing a stylish sense of the drama inherent in the blues but her stage performances, while commanding and impressive, occasionally went over the top in histrionics.

Lucille Bogan was a fine, down-to-earth singer. (Most blues collectors treasure her explicit version of *Shave 'Em Dry* which even today remains too hot for commercial release on a major label.) Hociel Thomas played piano to good effect but as a singer was never in the same class as her better-known relative, Sippie Wallace. And there was Hattie McDaniel who achieved lasting fame by becoming the first black actress to win an Oscar (for her performance in the 1939 film, *Gone With The Wind*).

Then there were the double acts, those vaudeville entertainers all of whom were influenced by jazz and the blues: the great Butterbeans and Susie with their honestly vulgar *I Wanna Hot Dog For My*

Roll; Coot Grant and Sox Wilson; Buck and Bubbles; and Liza Green and Ann Johnson. All these artists made excellent records which offer tantalising hints of their stage performances.

One artist who began her career singing the blues in cabaret and later moved confidently onto the stages of Broadway and London's West End, the movies and TV was Alberta Hunter (1895–1984). The eleven-year old Alberta's debut was at Dago Frank's, one of Chicago's least salubrious whorehouses, where she sang for the girls, their pimps, and their customers. Moving on, and fractionally upwards, she next sang in Hugh Hoskins' saloon. Soon she was on her way again and now found that she had an audience who followed her through a succession of saloons and cafes where she performed with other singers, among them the delightful Florence Mills and Ada Smith, better known as Bricktop, who became the toast of between-wars Paris.

Alberta Hunter hit the bigtime at the Dreamland Cafe on Chicago's South Side where she sang with King Oliver's band. One of the songs she performed there was her own composition *Down Hearted Blues*. Bessie Smith's version of this song became a best-selling record, eclipsing Alberta's own recording. Through the 1920s and early 1930s, Alberta recorded with many leading jazzmen of the day: Fletcher Henderson, Eubie Blake, Armstrong, Bechet and Fats Waller among them. In London she was so successful that she was offered the part of Queenie in the Drury Lane production of Kern and Hammerstein's *Showboat*, playing opposite Paul Robeson. This was the 1928–29 season and there were several more successes for her in London in the 1930s. She played the top nightspots, recorded sophisticated songs of the period, played the Dorchester Hotel with Jack Jackson's band and appeared in a dramatic (and somewhat out-of-place) sequence in the early British musical film *Radio Parade of 1935*.

Alberta Hunter's recordings of the late-1930s and early-1940s include excellent versions of *Down Hearted Blues*, *Chirpin' The Blues* and *Yelpin' The Blues* on which she is accompanied by Charlie Shavers (tp), Buster Bailey (cl) and Lil Hardin Armstrong (p). Her voice is powerful and confident and she displays a fine awareness of the nuances of a lyric (especially when she was responsible for the words herself). On *Someday, Sweetheart* she demonstrates one of her

Alberta Hunter – powerful authority.

trademarks, the drawing out of certain syllables with a controlled, subtle vibrato.

In 1940, accompanied by pianist Eddie Heywood, she recorded her theme, *My Castle's Rockin'*, and a superb interpretation of *The Love I Have For You*. Both songs are her own, yet are remarkably dissimilar, thus indicating the breadth of her abilities as songwriter and performer. On *The Love I Have For You*, a moving ballad, she sings with the effortless ease of a singer at the top of her profession. Alberta the singer's voice is in perfect shape for the dramatic bending of notes demanded by Alberta the composer. Her ringing contralto belied her tiny frame and she could belt out a song with the power needed to still the rowdy audiences of her chosen milieu.

In 1954, at the age of sixty, Alberta retired from show business and took up a career in nursing. Jazz writer and record producer Chris Albertson was able to persuade her into the studios to record two albums in 1961 but she stayed at her new profession, content with bringing a different kind of ease to her fellow human beings. Then, in 1977, her employers caught onto the fact that the diminutive Nurse Hunter was eighty-two and insisted that she should retire. She did, but only from nursing. Her renewed singing career is dealt with later in this book.

In the first quarter of the twentieth century, blues singers found an ever-growing audience in rural areas, in towns and cities throughout the American South and also in the south-western states. As we have seen, the best of them attracted attention much further afield and began influencing black singers across the nation, many of whom were also from backgrounds as diverse as America's white population.

During this same period, once again focussing upon New Orleans, the impact of the richly varied musical forms on young black men and women came from all kinds of performance. Formal dances and shows were far from being the sole source of music. Dance-halls, drinking joints and whorehouses, all provided music along with the other kinds of entertainment for which they were primarily designed. Citizens were also serenaded by beggars and street-vendors and children who sang in the streets for pennies. These youngsters performed in the hope of attracting money from passers-by who were either intent on a good time, or were staggering homewards having already had one.

It was as a member of an informal singing group that Louis Armstrong first performed in public. In time he would become the first truly great jazz musician, bringing to the music trumpet playing of dazzling technical virtuosity, linked to innovative musical ideas. But he began as a singer and, throughout his long career, singing remained an integral part of his performance. In the twilight of that career, when he had passed from being a jazz musician to become the most universally accepted artist America has ever produced, he sang on when his trumpet playing had suffered with the inevitable encroachment of age.

As a singer, Louis Armstrong (*c.*1898–1971) had a voice with qualities which rendered him wholly unsuitable in any other musical form. In the blues, content takes precedence over technique; in jazz, content is also important but so too are other facets which can be heard in Louis Armstrong's work from the beginning of his recorded output. His warm humanity and intense musical sensitivity was clearly evident in every performance. His enormous all-embracing influence still pervades every corner of the jazz world and is never more apparent than in his influence on singers and singing. It has been observed that Louis's singing is an extension of his trumpet playing; on the contrary, his playing echoes his vocal exhortations. Just as he did with his playing, Louis created a new concept with his vocalising. Unquestionably, his is the first true and complete jazz voice which he uses instrumentally, floating through the chord progressions, as if on his horn, with a beautifully veiled and throaty voice. Singing was never the same after his initial impact. Countless singers of varied styles took inspiration from his unique rhythmic phrasing. Among them were Cab Calloway and Billie Holiday, while Bing Crosby adopted a freer, more relaxed approach after coming under Armstrong's spell.

Louis Armstrong – amazing innovation.

The earliest recorded example of Armstrong's singing was captured on the Fletcher Henderson version of *Everybody Loves My Baby* in 1925. It was not until 1926, however, when he recorded the classic *Heebie Jeebies* with his Hot Five that Louis's singing was heard to any real effect. Whether or not his scat improvisations, in which rhythmic vocalised syllables replace words, was an impromptu interpretation or a predetermined adaptation may never be known for sure, but certainly *Heebie Jeebies*, with its rough but joyous scat vocal, was a singularly successful and influential recording. It was followed by numerous examples of this new, raw but exciting sound: *Skid Dat De Dat*, where Kid Ory's trombone and the clarinet of Johnny Dodds respond to Louis's vocal calls, and *I'm Not Rough* where, inspired by Lonnie Johnson's accompanying guitar, he gives a splendid vocal and instrumental performance.

Another early recording of note is *Georgia Grind*. Louis and Lil Armstrong sing two choruses apiece, giving some indication of the double act with which they successfully entertained audiences in Chicago. On *Big Butter And Egg Man* May Alix's lacklustre singing is totally eclipsed by Armstrong's spoken commentary which astonishingly outswings all but his own cornet solo. His 1927 recording of *Hotter Than That* has one of the great jazz vocal choruses which he scats in a tremendously exciting and adventurous fashion.

By the end of the 1920s Louis's vocalising began gradually to take on surprising contradictions. Some of the roughness disappeared and a much mellower sound was discernible. James Lincoln Collier's study of Louis suggests that growths on the vocal chords may have contributed to the gravelly sound, while occasional surgical shavings, eventually abandoned, temporarily softened the voice. On *Monday Date*, recorded with Earl Hines in 1928, he sings with a honeyed quality which echoes the sounds of the white crooners of the day. Indeed, on *My Sweet*, recorded in 1930, there are even signs of a Jolson influence. These are the first indications of Armstrong's future ballad style. He gives a tender interpretation of *I Can't Give You Anything But Love* and excels in his gloriously rearranged phrasing on *Body And Soul*. Similarly interesting and imaginative is his free use of the lyric on *Stardust*. On a somewhat abstract *Song Of The Vipers*, recorded in Europe in 1934, Louis predates by several decades those singers who would merge voice with instrumentation and use it as a section sound.

Few singers could interpret a popular song better than Louis Armstrong and this becomes increasingly obvious as the 1930s roll on. *Just A Gigolo* and *Sweethearts On Parade* are two mediocre songs given undue respectability by Armstrong's strong, poignant vocal interpretation. Three good songs, *I'm Confessin'*, *You Can Depend On Me* and *Keeping Out Of Mischief Now*, receive majestic treatment as does *When Your Lover Has Gone* which he performs with sublime magnificence.

Another song with which Armstrong achieved considerable success was Fats Waller's *Ain't Misbehavin'*, which he sang in the Broadway show 'Hot Chocolates' and in his nightclub act at Connie's Inn in 1931. At this time Louis was often backed by pedestrian bands that rarely interfered with his ability to transform a trite song into a thing of beauty. This is evident on his recordings of *Honey Don't You Love Me Anymore?* and *Dusky Stevedore*. His unhurried vocals combine elegant phrasing and gravel voice; all this, allied to a potent stage presence and sense of showmanship, made him an entertainer second to none. Time after time throughout the 1930s, Armstrong recorded definitive versions of popular songs, shaping them into pure jazz: *Thanks A Million, Eventide, Jubilee, I Double Dare You, You're A Lucky Guy* – the list is endless. On *I Hate To Leave You Now* he again changes a trite ballad into a superb vocal performance.

Not surprisingly, Armstrong's vocal style developed in parallel with his trumpet style. Firstly, the amazing innovator of the 1920s followed by the brilliant exhibitionist, and finally the assured, sober, middle-range showman who delighted the world.

The years he spent fronting his various All Stars groups have been damned with faint praise by the critics, yet they were extremely successful in presenting a jazz singer to a far wider audience than that usually afforded such an artist. This period also brought accusations of Uncle Tomism which were especially unfair. However much his rolling eyes and mugging might have offended black consciousness of the 1950s and 1960s, Louis was doing neither more nor less than he had done in the previous three decades. Now, more than ever before, he was the Entertainer; politics were for others.

Louis had huge popular successes: *Rockin' Chair*, on which he duetted with Jack Teagarden, and *Blueberry Hill* in the 1940s, *Mack*

The Knife in the 1950s, *Hello Dolly* and *It's A Wonderful World* in the 1960s, and many others in between. The jazz content of the accompaniment may have been thin but that criticism could rarely be levelled at his singing. Through these years his was jazz vocalising at its best, gaining in strength and subtlety – a fact unacknowledged by those who concentrated upon decrying the admitted lack of variety in the All Stars' performances.

Jack Teagarden apart, Louis had many successful encounters with other singers. Ella Fitzgerald's warmth and purity of style were perfectly complemented by Louis's even greater warmth and disarming humour on a number of occasions; humour was always to the fore in his duets with Bing Crosby; then there were the songs with the Mills Brothers; and through the All Stars years there were regular encounters with the band's vocalist, big-voiced Velma Middleton who also suffered at the hands of the critics. With hindsight it is difficult to understand why. In such performances as the humorous *That's My Desire* and *Baby It's Cold Outside* the pair ably continued the black vaudeville tradition of double acts.

Louis Armstrong's singing, like his trumpet playing, produced a stream of copyists (and an even longer string of out-and-out impressionists). After a while it appeared that every trumpet player in jazz was growling out gruff vocals. In the main they were poor but some can be singled out for their individualistic adaptation of his style: white New Orleaneans Louis Prima and Wingy Manone, two exuberant personalities both of whom were popular along New York's 52nd Street in the 1930s, Manone having an unlikely hit with *Isle Of Capri*. As well as the more obvious instrumental influence of Louis on their work, Roy Eldridge and Hot Lips Page were also affected (Page will be dealt with later) while perhaps the most interesting of all is Henry 'Red' Allen (1908–1967) whose erratic singing technique echoes his own adaptation of the Armstrong instrumental style. Allen's 1966 album 'Feeling Good' contains typical examples of this feature of his work.

The songs performed by Louis Armstrong, and by the blues singers of the classic period, came from a variety of sources. Many were 'traditional', a loose term covering numerous works which stemmed from one or another of the many threads which intertwined in popular music across the end of the nineteenth century. Some were trivial songs churned out by hacks who built upon musical forms they only barely understood. Others were formalised versions of songs which had been in the public domain for decades. Some, of course, were original and even inspired.

Among the black songwriters who came to prominence on the wave of popular interest in the blues were W.C. Handy, Spencer Williams, Clarence Williams, Chris Smith and Perry Bradford.

By the early-1920s there was a revival of interest in the music of black Americans. Among the songs which found their way onto the Broadway stage and into the homes of millions through records and sheet music were *The Memphis Blues, Beale Street Blues* and *The St Louis Blues* (Handy), *Basin Street Blues, I Ain't Got Nobody* (Spencer Williams), *Baby Won't You Please Come Home* (Clarence Williams), *Way Down Yonder In New Orleans, After You've Gone* (Henry Creamer and Turner Layton).

An enormously popular show, first staged on Broadway in 1921, was 'Shuffle Along'. This all-black production was also significant in restoring black performers to stages along the 'Great White Way' after a gap of more than a decade. The music and lyrics for this show were written by Eubie Blake and Noble Sissle and its star was Gertrude Saunders, perhaps best remembered for her sexual skirmishes with Bessie Smith's wayward husband Jack Gee. She was typical of black show singers whose sorties into the blues world are now rather laughable. Her versions of *Daddy Won't You Please Come Home* and *I'm Craving For That Kind Of Love* miss the essential drama of the blues. Also from 'Shuffle Along' came *I'm Just Wild About Harry* and its performance by Florence Mills, who took over from Gertrude Saunders, boosted this beautiful young woman to stardom although her tragically early death in 1927, while still in her twenties, robbed show business of one of its most talented stars. Among the many artists who appeared in one or another production of 'Shuffle Along' and who found later fame were Adelaide Hall, Lottie Gee, Josephine Baker, Paul Robeson, Lucille Hegamin and Eva Taylor.

The show's composers were also talented performers and the

double act of Sissle and Blake was enormously popular. Sissle's singing style was somewhat dated, harking back to the bland raggy style of those turn-of-the-century productions by Johnson, Cole and Johnson. Blake played excellent piano, both ragtime and stride, and could turn his hand more than adequately to the show tunes for which he wrote the music. Among Blake's other compositions, this time working with lyricist Andy Razaf, was *Memories Of You* from the show 'Blackbirds of 1930'. Blake later fell into obscurity, although *I'm Just Wild About Harry* enjoyed a new lease of life as Harry Truman's presidential campaign song in 1948. Late in the 1960s, Blake returned to public performances and soon gained an enthusiastic following. He recorded extensively, including a 1969 session with his old partner, Noble Sissle, which revived many of the songs of their glory days. He played festivals and concerts throughout the country and, in 1983, entered everyone's list of favourite quotations when, on the occasion of his 100th birthday, he remarked: 'If I'd known I was going to live this long, I would've taken better care of myself'. He died a few days later, one of the few ragtime pianists to benefit from the resurgence of interest in this musical form more than three-quarters of a century after its original stirrings.

The abbreviated career of Florence Mills made way for another entertainer who was welcomed onto the Broadway stage by white audiences who were responding enthusiastically to black culture as the Harlem Renaissance took hold of intellectual imaginations. She was Ethel Waters, who was born in Pennsylvania to a twelve-year old victim of a rapist.

The early years of Ethel Waters (1900–77) barely overcame this disastrous start and she entered into a doomed marriage when only thirteen. Four years later, in Baltimore, she entered vaudeville and sang W.C. Handy's *The St Louis Blues*, apparently becoming the first woman to sing the song publicly. During the following years she gained a substantial following and established a reputation as a fine blues singer. Unlike many of her contemporaries, Ethel Waters had a wide-ranging talent. By the mid-1920s she was a favourite of New York's nightclubbers and was responsible for the popularity of *Dinah* and *Travellin' All Alone*. Her recording debut was in 1921, thus predating the established blues giants Bessie Smith and Ma

Rainey. Her recordings, and those of Alberta Hunter, helped restore the troubled fortunes of Harry Pace, the first black owner of a record company. Ethel Waters regularly performed with the backing of established jazz artists and several up-and-coming newcomers to the jazz scene. Fletcher Henderson, James P. Johnson, Coleman Hawkins and Duke Ellington were among them and, significantly, she was one of the first black singers to work with white accompanists: Benny Goodman, Tommy Dorsey, Jack Teagarden.

In the 1930s she became a leading performer at New York's Cotton Club, the Harlem establishment on the northeast corner of 142nd Street and Lenox Avenue, which was clubland's pinnacle of success for black entertainers. Entertainment aside, however, the only other places for blacks at the club were as cooks, waitresses and the like.

Ethel Waters' fame spread internationally, thanks to her recordings, and when she introduced the Harold Arlen-Ted Koehler song, *Stormy Weather* at the club in 1933 she evoked in her listeners a depth of understanding that penetrated even the sensibilities of those who regarded visits to Harlem as little more than a means of keeping in the cultural swim. For Waters, the song allowed her to do something she could not otherwise accomplish. As she wrote in her sometimes self-lacerating autobiography, *His Eye Is On The Sparrow*, 'I was singing the story of my misery and confusion, of the misunderstandings in my life I couldn't straighten out, the story of the wrongs and outrages done to me by people I had loved and trusted'. As the song was written by white songsmiths and technically is not strictly a blues, this demonstrates an essential ingredient in the blues which was already permeating popular music – emotional universality.

Of the three major jazz voices of the 1920s, Bessie Smith, Louis Armstrong and Ethel Waters, it is the latter who must be regarded as the most influential of all. Bessie Smith is the yardstick by which all blues singers are measured; Louis Armstrong, the innovator, created a style and was *the* original jazz voice; but Ethel Waters transcended most positively and effectively the wider boundaries of American popular song. So effective was she that blues and jazz singers, vaudeville artists the popular entertainers alike came under her spell. It was Waters, even more so than Armstrong, who demonstrated

Ethel Waters – most influential

that jazz style was adaptable to popular song. Her own style was culled not only from black traditions but also from the white tradition. For example, she had much in common with white vaudevilleans Nora Bayes and Sophie Tucker. As she developed, distinct Jolson traits were also discernible in her accenting of words.

Dozens of hopeful black singers were inspired by the sophistication of her lilting voice, stylistically opposed as it was to the roughness of Ma Rainey and more intimate than the vaudevillean delivery of Mamie Smith. Equally, she inspired white artists who aspired to the mantle of the jazz singer. They could identify more readily with her sophistication than with the raw emotion of Bessie Smith. Yet, in a very real sense, Ethel Waters was a performer who absorbed important elements of the blues and jazz idioms in order to enhance her singing style without ever becoming wholly and unmistakably a part of either tradition. Ironically, although most influential of the three vocal giants of the 1920s, she is now the least remembered. This is because her stylistic descendants proved so very successful in learning and adapting her style to their own requirements that they were thought to have been either original spirits or had learned elsewhere.

The list of singers influenced by Ethel includes those who were performing when she came along and others who followed, and it reads like a roll of honour: Connee Boswell, Ruth Etting, Sophie Tucker, Adelaide Hall, Billie Holiday, Ivie Anderson, Mildred Bailey, Helen Humes, Lee Wiley, Lena Horne, Pearl Bailey, Ella Fitzgerald. All these singers, and more, have stylistic attributes which originate in the artistry of Ethel Waters.

Originally billed on the TOBA circuit as 'Sweet Mama Stringbean', Ethel's humour and brightness quickly captured an adoring audience – much to the chagrin of some of the other leading blues singers of the time.

Ethel Waters could sing a blues beautifully, but more often her repertoire consisted of popular songs of the day. Her diction was exceptional, although her phrasing could be extremely stylised. For example, her use of the rolled 'r' became tiresome when overdone. Bessie Smith and Louis Armstrong rarely made a record that was less than good, but Waters often recorded inferior songs with banal lyrics which even she could not overcome. At her best, however, she was superb. Her 1925 recording of *Shake That Thing* featured the Ethel Waters of the TOBA-circuit days, sensual and buoyant; *No Man's Mama* has a bright, spirited, and rather white, sound to it; on *Sweet Man* the two sides of her nature converge and she sings with beguiling charm, totally capturing the listener's attention. When she recorded *Heebie Jeebies* in 1926 she produced a jazz performance of considerable merit although this type of swinging number was something of a rarity as her forte was the emotional, dramatic performance.

The pre-minent black singer of the early-1930s, Ethel Waters popularised many songs (especially *Dinah* on which she rephrased the lyrics, in the process fashioning a jazz performance of considerable charm). It was her polished phrasing and the fine quality of her conversational delivery which delighted jazz musicians of the era. In these years, the 1930s, the matured style of Ethel Waters was unsurpassed. Her recordings of such songs as *You've Seen Harlem At Its Best, Stormy Weather, Miss Otis Regrets, Moonglow, Happiness Is Just A Guy Called Joe* and *You Can't Stop Me From Loving You* may be highly stylised but nevertheless stand as superb examples of her interpretative gifts.

She enjoyed a later career as a dramatic actress on Broadway and appeared in several films, most notably *Pinky* and *The Member Of The Wedding* and she also starred in the TV series, *Beulah*.

The simplistic historical myth which says that jazz was created in New Orleans around 1900 continues with the music travelling upriver to Chicago around 1920. Once again, there is an element of justification in this inaccurate proposal because Chicago serves as a useful focus of attention for the development of jazz during the 1920s.

In the years between America's entry into World War 1 and 1921 a massive migration of blacks took place. Intent on leaving the South, they were attracted by the prospect of the industrialised north. It was the obvious place to head for, given that work was plentiful, there was government encouragement, and much exhortation along

53

the grapevine and in newspapers. The Chicago *Defender* was influential in urging southern blacks to come to Chicago but not merely to better themselves financially. The editorial exhortations carried a more spiritual message: 'I beg of you my brethren.... Your neck has been in the yoke.... To die from the bite of frost is far more glorious than that of the mob'. More practically, perhaps, there really were jobs to be had. Chicago was a major transport centre and, around its railroads, roads and canals, industry had built up with huge stockyards, meat-packing plants and the like. Job vacancies in the stockyards alone were touted at 50,000 and while this figure sounds mightily optimistic, it conveys the city's appeal as a place where work, pay and freedom were there for the taking. The South Side became known as the Black Belt. From 26th Street down to 63rd Street, spanning Dearborn Street in the west and Cottage Grove Avenue to the east, blacks made Chicago a major centre although, given the staggering rate of growth of the city, they represented less than five per cent of the population.

Just as New Orleans had been a wide-open city, so too Chicago had an 'anything goes' policy, sometimes unofficially, occasionally (as when Big Bill Thompson first became mayor in 1914) with official sanction. With work for all, pay was high and in its wake came entertainment. Again, there was prostitution, a recurrence of the unfortunate corollary from which jazz has forever suffered; there was drinking and, because Prohibition had come in at the beginning of 1920, that meant there was also crime. Illegal drinking joints, bootleggers, the Al Capone-led gangsters, the newly arrived migrants, black and white, all blended together. Perhaps the blending was not always easy, but at least it was done to musical accompaniment.

The 1920s were known in America as 'The Jazz Age' but in the real sense this was a misuse of the word 'jazz'. The Jazz Age was indicative of an era of abandonment in attitudes towards life, morals, sexual mores, drinking and drug-taking. The popular music of the era was bright and brittle. The songs were lively, often frenetic, the lyrics frequently daring but little of that which reached the wider public was jazz and the songs were not sung by jazz singers.

Nevertheless, the music of the age was quite certainly what the uninformed public thought of as 'jazzy'. For those who cared to

54

look, however, real jazz abounded in the city and many singers obtained work there, whether passing through or as residents; among them were many country blues singers whose work now began to change.

The search by record companies in the 1920s for more and yet more black performers to satisfy the newly-realised market, brought to the studios a cornucopia of black talent mainly from the South. Artistic styles ranged from the almost unintelligible hollers of street evangalists, such as Blind Willie Johnson and Gary Davis, to the spritely sophistication of circuit entertainers like Frankie 'Half Pint' Jaxon and Papa Charlie Jackson.

Regional influences played a considerable part in forging the path taken by the blues; influences largely transmitted through the medium of the phonograph record.

One of the earliest and most important street singers to record came from Texas. Blind Lemon Jefferson (1897–1929) sang blues that were raw and rugged, echoing sounds of the field hollers and work songs he had heard in his youth. Jefferson was the repository of songs and styles he had learned while touring through the southern states and in his early days on the streets of Dallas. His repertoire, which included both the sacred and the profane, was sung in a high-pitched voice. Some of his songs contained personal recollections of life as he had lived it:

Slippin' 'roun' the corner runnin' up alleys too
I went slippin' 'roun' the corner runnin' up alleys too
Watchin' my woman tryin' to see what she goin' to do.

Although Jefferson was a fat, dirty and dissolute man, his eighty-odd records, made between 1926 and the end of his life are a moving and sensitive document of the life he led and are replete with stark imagery, bluntly conveyed:

Peach orchard Mama you swore nobody'd pick your
    fruit but me (×2)
I found three kid men shakin' down your peaches free.

Blind Lemon Jefferson died as he had lived, on the streets. His frozen, snow-covered body was found there, his now-silent guitar beside him.

Another early Texan singer was Texas Alexander (c.1880–c.1955) who recorded in New York for OKeh. He had a warm voice and his blues singing, with its field holler characteristics, was filled with country imagery:

> I laid down last night I was tryin' to take my rest (×2)
> Then my mind kept a ramblin' like the wild geese in the west.

Among later good blues artists from Texas were T-Bone Walker and Lightnin' Hopkins who will be dealt with elsewhere.

While Jefferson and Alexander were typical of the early Texas singers, Charlie Patton (1887–1934) was the dean of the Mississippi Delta lineage. Patton had a deep, gruff voice and numerous great blues singers have continued to follow the trail he blazed: Robert Johnson, Son House, Bukka White, Muddy Waters, Howling Wolf and Elmore James are among them.

Blind Blake (c.1890–c.1933) was born in Florida and typifies the blind singer to be found at street corners, at picnics and fish-fries. There was a light, raggy quality to his guitar playing, and his nasal singing tone echoed the loneliness of his kind as he stood on Chicago's State Street in the 1920s:

> Come on boys let's do that messin' around this morning
> Come on boys lets have some doggone fun.

Blake's singing style helped shape the blues of the 1930s and among the fine singers he partially influenced can be listed Big Bill Broonzy, Blind Gary Davis, Blind Boy Fuller and Josh White.

Another state which produced early influential singers was Georgia. One of the finest was Peg Leg Howell (1888–1966), a country singer with considerable feeling who, along with 'his Gang', worked the streets and parks of Atlanta. Other good Georgia blues singers included Barbecue Bob and his brother Laughing Charlie. The career of Georgia's most distinguished male singer, Georgia Tom Dorsey, is examined later.

New Orleans is not particularly noted as a blues centre but the

Crescent City was home to some singers, and best of all was the legendary Lonnie Johnson (c.1889–1970) who began his career playing and singing with his family on street corners. During World War 1 a 'flu epidemic killed off thirteen of his immediate relatives and he left New Orleans. He toured the country and in 1917 was entertaining American troops in London in a musical revue. On his return to America he began working out of St Louis where he played guitar with Charlie Creath's band in dance halls and on the riverboat 'S.S. St Paul'. In 1925 he entered and won a blues contest. Jesse Stone, the local representative for OKeh, heard him and within days Johnson had made his first records. He was soon one of the country's most popular blues artists both as a guitar accompanist and as singer in his own right. For the next two years OKeh issued a Johnson record every six weeks. As well as singing the blues, he recorded excellent instrumentals with Duke Ellington, Louis Armstrong and McKinney's Cotton Pickers. He also provided extremely fine accompaniment for Texas Alexander and Victoria Spivey. In 1929 he recorded some exceptional guitar duets with Eddie Lang.

Johnson sang with a bitter directness, usually about loneliness and lost love. An early example of his work is the despairing *When You Fall For Someone That's Not Your Own:*

Blues and trouble they walk hand in hand (×2)
But you never had no trouble 'til you fall for the wife of
    another man
When it begins raining you're looking out your window pane
    (×2)
Thinking of that other man's wife it's enough to drive you
    insane
You say blues and trouble have followed you all the days of
    your life
Blues and trouble they have followed you all the days of your
    life
You never had no trouble 'til you fall for another man's wife
A married woman in sweet the sweetest woman ever was born
    (×2)
Only thing wrong with her every time she has to go back
    home.

Apart from being a superb blues guitarist, Johnson's diction was distinct, his singing tone mellow. Initially, he sang the blues but as he matured he began to include more and more blues ballads in his repertoire. He composed most of his own material and was possibly the first rhythm balladeer. A line of influence can be traced from Johnson through a host of singers including Big Bill Broonzy, Percy Mayfield and Charles Brown. Johnson's vocal talent was complemented by his guitar work, and here too his influence stretches through the years: T-Bone Walker, Lowell Fulson, B.B. King, and also in the work of jazz guitarists Teddy Bunn, Eddie Durham and even Charlie Christian. More than any other singer of his time, Johnson brought urban sophistication to the country blues. He worked regularly until an accident and a stroke incapacitated him.

Alongside the blues singers were the blues songsters. These were entertainers who used the blues, work songs and minstrel tunes to augment their repertoires and they sang of notable events and of folk heroes. Rabbit Brown of New Orleans was one, John Hurt, Furry Lewis and John Jackson of Mississippi, Mance Lipscombe of Texas, Jesse Fuller of Georgia, Pink Anderson of South Carolina were all adepts, but best remembered of all was Huddie Ledbetter, better known as Leadbelly, of Louisiana.

Leadbelly (1889–1949) was a violent, brooding man, qualities his singing clearly portrayed. His voice held the very taste of the prison life he knew so well. Hard and rough, with a cruel edge to it, his performance of Leroy Carr's *How Long, How Long Blues* was in stark contrast to the urban charm of the composer's rendition. The final years of Leadbelly's life: tours of Europe, Library of Congress recordings and all, are in striking contrast to his early days. Similarly unlikely is the long afterlife of two of his most famous songs: *Irene Goodnight* and *Rock Island Line*, most often performed by singers who would have run a mile from contact with Leadbelly in his youth.

Those singers who worked the TOBA-circuits were many and varied. One such performer who made some early recordings was Cow Cow Davenport (1894–1955), a rolling, barrelhouse piano player and one of the originators of the boogie woogie piano style. There was a warm and happy quality to his voice. He learned his trade in the tent shows and wrote many songs, including *Cow Cow*

Blues and also claimed *Mama Don't Allow It* and *I'll Be Glad When You're Dead You Rascal You!* Davenport and his wife, Dora Carr, were the first husband and wife vaudeville team to appear on race records. Among singers he influenced were such notable musicians as Pinetop Smith and Cripple Clarence Lofton.

Frankie 'Half Pint' Jaxon (1895-unk.) was a typical small-time show business performer. He moved easily from night clubs to vaudeville, from jazz band to folk group. He also danced, acted as emcee, and was a stand-up comic. He worked with many famous jazzmen including King Oliver, Bennie Moten and Freddie Keppard. His speciality was female impersonation and his shrill singing voice is easily identifiable. He recorded a number of times with Tampa Red and various jazz groups during the 1930s and early-1940s but retired from show business to work for the government. Jaxon (his real name was probably Jackson) had a gift for extending the meaning of a lyric far beyond the often simplistic level imagined by the writer. This added quality (for it is more than mere innuendo) together with the natural exuberance of his performances, warrant a more important place in the history of black music than he has ever been accorded.

By the end of the 1920s the musical trends which had spawned the blues, ragtime and jazz had changed the character of the original. The blues, which continued as a mainly black musical form, was widespread throughout the nation, although necessarily concentrated in areas with a predominantly black population. Thus the South remained a stronghold, as did such northern enclaves as the black quarter of Chicago. Ragtime, with its relatively rigid structure proved to have only limited appeal for popular songwriters and jazz musicians alike and faded rapidly early in the decade. By the beginning of the 1930s, it was a musical curiosity remembered by few and played almost not at all.

If the blues was limited in its popular appeal at the start of the 1930s, and if ragtime was in a state of suspended animation, jazz was about to enter an era of unprecedented popularity. Personal appearances and records played their part in this surge of popularity, of course, but so too did an explosion in popular culture which affected almost every American. In part, this explosion came about through the movies, for this was also Hollywood's Golden Era, but most of all it was due to the box which stood in the corner of living rooms across the nation. Regardless of its owner's status, race, creed, colour or musical preference – this box brought entertainment of all kinds, and music in particular, straight into the home. It was, of course, the radio.

3 Crooners, Canaries and Lady Day

New decade or not, the 1930s found racial divisions within show business as sharply-edged as before. The relatively sophisticated Broadway show, with its overtones of European musical styles, had become largely the province of white artists with blacks almost totally excluded. The vaudeville circuit-based black artists incorporated more overtly black music in their material as their audiences were usually exclusively black. These two broad bands, the white and the black, still cross-fertilised thanks to recordings and the positive interest artists displayed in one another's work (albeit sometimes for financial gain rather than purely aesthetic reasons).

White performers found commercial acceptance more readily and adjusted their style and the content of their repertoires accordingly while many black artists continued using and adapting the blues tradition through the new decade. The blues changed, of course, if in no other way than by recognition in lyrics of the contemporary social and economic scene. Although there were substantial geographic and social areas of America which flourished in the early 1930s, there were numerous regions, especially those in the rural heartland, which were crippled by economic hardship. The Great Depression struck at the mid-West, sending shock waves into all areas of industry and commerce. The effect differed however. In certain parts of the nation, especially in the Deep South among blacks and poor whites, there was an air of faint bewilderment at the

61

clamour being raised in some quarters. For them it always had been depression. In other parts of the nation, not necessarily considered by geographic area, times were not all that bad. The myth of middle-class businessmen killing themselves in droves leads to the impression that at the time of the Crash of '29 it was positively dangerous to walk through New York's financial district for fear of being hit by flying bodies as newly-bankrupted executives took a dive from the fortieth floor. It was never so; perhaps one or two men ended their lives in this way but the same could be said for almost any year. Someone is always going broke.

Nevertheless, the times, those of economic uncertainty, heartbreak and despair for many, did provide material suitable for incorporation in the lyrics of blues (and other) songs and their titles are indicative of their mood: *The Red Cross Store Blues, WPA Blues, Welfare Store* and *Buddy, Can You Spare A Dime?*.

Much more significant in the world of popular music during this period, however, was the development of radio. Just as records had spread throughout the 1920s so too had radio. The boom in radio was startling in the rate at which it both spread and grew. From virtually nothing in 1920 radio set ownership mushroomed until, in 1930, 14 million sets were owned and that figure would more than triple before 1940.

The little box in the corner became almost a member of the family and favourite programmes were followed slavishly. Of course, radio carried much more than just music. The range of broadcast material was extensive and when the fortunes of vaudeville theatres slumped in the early 1930s, the radio networks underwent a corresponding boom. Variety and comedy shows were soon a dominant feature of most radio stations' schedules. Eddie Cantor, Al Jolson and crooner Rudy Vallee were hugely popular, as were the Marx Brothers, Jack Benny, Fred Allen and George Burns and Gracie Allen. All these artists had regular shows sponsored by such household names as Lucky Strike, Maxwell House, Esso and Canada Dry. The content of the shows bore little relationship to what was happening in those parts of the land hit hardest by the Depression. Even during the banking crisis of 1933 millions listened to Amos 'n' Andy as if unaware of the disaster lurking over their heads. There was also a gradual emergence of awareness that radio was a useful political tool.

President Herbert Hoover remarked to Rudy Vallee, 'If you can sing a song that would make people forget their troubles and the Depression, I'll give you a medal'. It was Hoover's successor, Franklin D. Roosevelt, who turned to radio as a means of drawing the people together, and he used it as a powerful means of gaining popular support for his proposals and enhancing his political power. This boom in radio, then, hit theatres and records but by the mid-1930s, the record industry recovered, using the slogan: 'Music you want *when* you want it'. The beneficiaries of the surge of popularity in radio and records were predominantly the white entertainers and many of them became national stars for, despite the fragmentary nature of American radio, most local stations welcomed the networking of shows from the main centres of entertainment. One such early beneficiary of this fame was Vaughn De Leath who became the first woman singer to gain widespread recognition. Her repertoire included popular songs of the day, among them Sissle and Blake's *I'm Just Wild About Harry* and she also sang blues songs. In the South, singer Kate Smith, a lady of decidedly ample proportions, actually competed successfully with Amos 'n' Andy. Among the songs Kate popularised were *Please Don't Talk About Me When I'm Gone* and Irving Berlin's *God Bless America*.

But radio was not the only entertainment area which prospered in this period; so too did Harlem. During the early nineteenth century blacks in New York moved slowly north and west from the Five Points ghetto and as they did so white Americans uprooted and headed even further north into Harlem. As the century unrolled, Harlem became a desirable suburb and home to the affluent. Then, as New York City expanded with the influx of vast numbers of immigrants from the Old World, Harlem came under pressure. Italians moved there, as did Jews who could now afford to move out of the Lower East Side wherein they had made their first homes. Some blacks came to the edges of Harlem too. New York's black population expanded at about the same time as Chicago's, albeit at a slower pace. Even so, by 1920 there were more than 150,000 blacks in the city and many were poverty-wracked migrants from the Deep South. The already resident black population disapproved of these incomers and the whites were decidedly unhappy. As Leroy Ostransky has suggested, this general dismay stemmed from different attitudes: black New Yorkers thought the incomers compromised their position through their illiteracy, insanitary habits and a certain crudity of behaviour; white New Yorkers were more worried at the prospect of racial unrest, their fears fuelled by memories of riots in 1900 and 1905. As a result, whites and better-off blacks alike moved out and Harlem swiftly became almost exclusively black.

Black Harlem in the 1920s and 1930s was much more than merely a residential enclave and far from being the popular interpretation of a ghetto. The cultural and social life of the district was extraordinarily intense, with theatres, restaurants, saloons and night-spots of all kinds from the classiest up-market watering holes to dives where only the fearless, or foolish, dared venture.

An upsurge in black theatre and literature during the period led to the application of the term, 'Harlem Renaissance', even if this inaccurately implies a previous period when an advanced black culture had existed there. Although Harlem represented much more to blacks, white Americans treated the district as if it were some kind of zoo they could visit to look at curiously alien life forms without placing themselves in any danger of physical damage or intellectual degradation – for, despite some advances in attitudes, many whites still held a primitive view, and fear, of blacks. It was during this period that the Cotton Club became a favourite haunt of white sophisticates (or, at least, those who thought of themselves as sophisticated). There they could see beautiful scantily-clad black girls and dangerously erotic black male dancers; they could hear 'jungle music' played by black jazzmen and, of course, they were served by black waiters. But they did not have to share a table with blacks because the house rules initially restricted the club to white patrons. Integration at that level would have been too much and, anyway, the club was owned by whites. Gangsters they might have been, but they had a fine sense of the proprieties. In any event, it was more important to many visitors that they should be *seen*; to go further would have been unwarranted and possibly dangerous lily-gilding. A later change in the rules, pressed upon the owners by the local black community, was to some extent countered by high prices which effectively kept out blacks. In any event, they knew better than to cause trouble by going where they were not wanted.

Recent attention paid to the Cotton Club, thanks to the 1985 movie which bears its name, has suggested it was almost alone but it was, in fact, only one of a seemingly countless number of places where black music could be heard. There were, literally, hundreds of clubs, although the frequent name changes required to stay a step or two ahead of the law makes an accurate count next to impossible. There was Barron Wilkin's Exclusive Club and Small's Paradise; the Lenox Club where pianist Willie 'The Lion' Smith held court; Pod's and Jerry's Log Cabin where the young Billie Holiday appeared; the Hot Feet Club featured Fats Waller; the Sugar Cane had Ethel Waters; just about every jazzman of note sat in at the Rhythm Club's jam sessions; and Louis Armstrong startled jazzmen and fans alike from the bandstand at Connie's Inn which was also pricey. The district's leading dancehall was the Savoy Ballroom, the Home of Happy Feet, which was the 'jumpingest' place in town and, during the reign of Chick Webb and his Orchestra, woe betide any band which ventured there for a cutting contest. And then there was the Apollo Theatre which had opened as a burlesque theatre but twenty years on, in the mid-1930s, had become the city's, and the nation's, leading black vaudeville theatre. Across the Apollo's stage passed every black act of any consequence and its talent contests lifted such activities to heights undreamed of by promoters at any other venue. After falling on hard times, the Apollo eventually closed in the 1970s but reopened with a great fanfare (and a decidedly pop-orientated policy) in May 1985.

While all these venues resonate in the ears of jazzmen, the Cotton Club, with all its faults and latterday hype, remains the most evocative. It was here that Duke Ellington began a five-year residency in 1927 which boosted him to national fame, thanks to direct radio broadcasts. And, as we have seen, it was also the place from which Ethel Waters rose to prominence. Cab Calloway, Ellington's successor at the club, will be considered later.

The development of white singers during the early 1930s grew apace, encouraged as they were by the sheer volume of work available in radio and on records. These singers benefited from old prejudices as many sponsors of radio shows refused to allow black artists to promote their products. Among those who touched the fringes of jazz was one man who dominated the airwaves.

Harry Lillis Crosby (1904–77) picked up the nickname Bing

while still at school, which was where he began his career in music singing with the school jazz band. At university he met up with Al Rinker and the two men began singing duets. Soon abandoning their studies, Crosby and Rinker went west in the hope that Rinker's sister, the jazz singer Mildred Bailey, would help them find singing jobs. Crosby and Rinker made their first recording in 1926 and were soon hired by Paul Whiteman. Later the pair were joined by Harry Barris and adopted the name, the Rhythm Boys. In the late-1920s they became very popular with audiences and their first records with the Whiteman band were highly successful. Being part of the Whiteman organisation meant that they worked with some of the leading white jazzmen of the day: Joe Venuti, Eddie Lang, the Dorsey brothers and Bix Beiderbecke.

By this time, jazz was a recognized part of the American way of life, although little of the genuine article percolated through to the average white household. Jazz to the white masses still meant Al Jolson (who had made the 1927 movie *The Jazz Singer*), Paul Whiteman (who appeared in *The King Of Jazz*, a film made in 1930), George Gershwin (who composed *Rhapsody In Blue* which just about everyone seemed to believe was the definitive jazz composition), and entertainers like Ukelele Ike and Ted Lewis. The rise in popularity of the 'crooners' who benefited from the introduction of the microphone (which allowed them to sing softly, or croon) produced a rather motley crew. There were the good, the bad and the indifferent (and few things could be more indifferent than a not-very-good crooner): Gene Austin, Rudy Vallee, Russ Colombo and Whispering Jack Smith were among them but Bing Crosby was destined to eclipse them all. More than any other popular singer he completely mastered the new technique of singing through a microphone. He used it not to overpower but to permit a previously unheard intimacy between singer and listener.

Alongside Crosby other young crooners began recording with jazz-styled dance bands, among them the adenoidal Irving Kauffman and the ineffective Chick Bullock and Dick Robertson. The plummy-voiced Red McKenzie and pianist-singer Seger Ellis were in the forefront of these jazz-orientated singers but none had the quality of natural rhythm which Crosby possessed. Indeed, few singers had more influence upon American popular singing unless it

66

was his female counterpart and near-contemporary Connee Boswell. Crosby's original influences were the descendants of the minstrel show singers – Jolson and Ukelele Ike, and also the light-classical tenor John McCormack. On the other hand, Connee Boswell (c.1912–76), being New Orleans born and bred, had immediate access to the jazz sounds of that city. The veteran Chicago clarinetist Volly De Faut has suggested that Connee's phrasing originated from listening to the cornet of Emmett Hardy, whereas Connee acknowledged an early interest in the vocal qualities of Bessie Smith and opera singer Enrico Caruso (whose records, she claimed, taught her breath control). Another of her early interests was the blues. Connee began her recording career before entering her teenage, the song, *Cryin' Blues* being composed by her sister Martha. At an early age Connee contracted polio and ever afterwards was confined to a wheelchair.

Both Crosby and Connee Boswell quickly came to appreciate the rhythmic advances of Louis Armstrong and Ethel Waters. At heart, both Bing and Connee were two-beat singers, always most at ease within the Dixieland format in which they were immersed during their formative years. Connee and her sisters, Martha and Helvetia, created a form of close harmony that was quite unique and identifiably their own. Their work immeasurably advanced the style of other female vocal groups which included the Brox Sisters, the Ponce Sisters and the Williams Sisters.

Crosby, Rinker and Barris were working along similar lines. While with the Paul Whiteman organisation they created interest with their performances on such songs as *Mississippi Mud* and *I'm Coming Virginia*. Unlike the Boswell Sisters, who echoed the polyrhythmic harmonies of the New Orleans jazz bands, the Rhythm Boys clearly emulated the tighter lines of Bix, Frank Trumbauer and the Wolverines, with a considerable amount of minstrel hokum thrown in.

As individuals, Bing and Connee both showed obvious similarities of approach and phrasing. They both made extensive use of the sustained vowel sound using the 'oohs' and 'aahs' as points of entry to a lyric or as a re-entry to a phrase or verse. This gave both singers a very distinctive sound and is apparent from the lazy ease Crosby demonstrates on *Please* or *When The Blue Of The Night Meets The*

Gold Of The Day, or on his much more jazz-orientated versions of *Sweet Georgia Brown* and *My Honey's Lovin' Arms* recorded in the early 1930s. It is equally clear on his later recording of *Personality* with Eddie Condon's band which features the raunchy cornet of Wild Bill Davison and the almost over-exaggerated drumming of George Wettling.

In Connee Boswell's case, her use of the same vocal effects are typically in evidence on *Trust In Me* and *That Old Feeling* recorded with Ben Pollack's band in 1937 and on the album she made in the 1950s with the reconstituted Original Memphis Five.

Connee and Bing combined on many occasions to produce duets of considerable warmth and swing. One of the best examples being their recording of *Basin Street Blues* which has an excellent trombone introduction by Abe Lincoln; and *That's A Plenty* with a perfectly coordinated call-and-response from the singers.

Crosby influenced a whole generation of band singers while Boswell's easy, swinging phrasing influenced not only many later singers but some, like Mildred Bailey and Ruth Etting, who were already established but were unafraid to learn from a talented newcomer. They gained in rhythmic technique after hearing the quality of her phrasing.

A phenomenon peculiar to the Jazz Age and which lingered on into the 1930s was the 'torch singer'. This term still conjures up visions of sad-eyed young ladies sitting atop a piano, softly trilling a slightly risqué ballad. Among such singers were the famed Helen Morgan, and Libby Holman who suggestively rolled her eyes as she pouted her off-key renditions of *Moanin' Low* and *Am I Blue?*.

A true product of this brittle age of the good-time girl was Ruth Etting. With clever phrasing she attractively popularised such songs as *Ten Cents A Dance*, *It All Belongs To Me*, *Love Me Or Leave Me* and *Button Up Your Overcoat*. She was accompanied by many of the top studio jazz musicians of the day, among them Mannie Klein (tp), Rube Bloom (p) and Eddie Lang (g). Jazz writer Derrick Stewart-Baxter has reported that both Lucille Hegamin and Victoria Spivey expressed admiration for Ruth Etting's work.

Annette Hanshaw's saccharine-sweet voice was also prominent and she sounded quite acceptable when backed by such musicians as Joe Venuti (v), Vic Berton (d), the ever-present Eddie Lang and by

The Boswell Sisters – immeasurably advanced.

Adrian Rollini playing everything but the kitchen sink. Hanshaw cornered the market in breezy, happy-go-lucky songs such as *I Like What You Like* and *Ain't That A Grand and Glorious Feeling*. Usually ending her recordings with the coy tag line, 'that's all'. A minor resurgence of interest in her work occurred in the 1970s with the reissue of practically everything she had ever recorded with seemingly little regard for its intrinsic merits. Few of her contemporaries enjoyed a revival of any kind, let along such a wholesale programme of reisssues. Now barely recalled are Marion Harris, Jane Green, Lillian Roth, Margaret Young and Lee Morse, all of whom recorded pleasant if unexceptional numbers with jazz backing. Indeed, even vaudevilleans like Sophie Tucker and the outgoing Blossom Seeley cheerfully involved themselves with this type of music.

A number of popular composers and lyricists also attempted singing in the jazz idiom. There is recorded evidence of Harold Arlen's not-altogether successful attempts at jazz singing with the Duke Ellington Orchestra. Johnny Mercer and his easy Georgia drawl became quite proficient in the medium but the most successful of all was Hoagy Carmichael whose downhome voice was filled with unpretentious charm. His singing always perfectly complemented his own compositions. His early version of *Stardust*, with its echoes of Armstrong's phrasing, or the bluesy inflections on *Moon Country* and *Hong Kong Blues* are fine examples. His well-pitched but limited voice varied in shade, always sounding spontaneous and not at all effortful. He greatly influenced a small but continuing line of jazz-orientated singers stretching through to the present-day with Mose Allison, Dave Frishberg and Georgie Fame among them.

Perhaps the most successful, and certainly the most widely-accepted white singer from this tradition was the Texan trombone-player Jack Teagarden (1905–64). His trombone playing was a revelation to his contemporaries and he had no difficulty in finding work with such bands as that led by Ben Pollack with whom he worked for five years from 1928 (almost causing Glenn Miller, who was also with Pollack at this time, to pack his trombone away for ever).

Influenced by the blues singers of his home state, Teagarden sang with a sleepy drawl which assimilated the casual but assured

Jack Teagarden – lazy humour.

approach of Crosby's vocalising. Teagarden's was the linking voice between the blues and the popular singing style of Crosby. He was one of the few truly convincing male white singers in the jazz and blues idiom in the 1920s and 1930s. His blues chorus on Eddie Condon's *That's A Serious Thing*, recorded in 1929, is a superb example, as is his mellow interpretation on Paul Whiteman's *Nobody's Sweetheart Now* in 1935. That Teagarden was the perfect vocal foil to Louis Armstrong was clearly demonstrated on their numerous performances of Hoagy Carmichael's *Rockin' Chair* and on *Don't Stop Playing Those Blues, Boys*. His humour and easy delivery superbly complemented the hoarse declamatory charm of Louis's voice.

By virtue of his definitive performances, on which he demonstrates his superlative trombone technique and his lazy vocal charm, Teagarden made many jazz numbers his own: *I'm Coming Virginia, Aunt Hagar's Blues, If I Could Be With You One Hour Tonight, Stars Fell On Alabama, The Sheik Of Araby* and, especially, *Basin Street Blues*.

A female counterpart to Teagarden was Teddy Grace, who also assimilated the jazz and blues idiom in a convincing manner.

The benefits brought to American popular song through radio cannot be overstated while the effective linking up of regions and cities across the nation makes even less tenable than usual the isolation of individual centres as being especially significant in the development of jazz. Nevertheless, some places deserve special attention, sometimes for the major new waves which were generated, other times for their adherence to past times and musical styles.

In the country districts of the Deep South, the Mississippi Delta for example, life rolled on much as always. As indicated, depression was just a word used to describe a condition the black people here had always known and their music reveals this.

The country blues singers, many of whom effected the transition to urban blues singing demanded by changes in public taste, were numerous. So many were preserved on record that an impression is gained of record company executives hovering in every wayside saloon, on every street corner, and outside every prison farm in the South. Some of the relatively unknown singers thus recorded deserve their obscurity yet occasionally light up their performances with a superbly defined phrase or ingenious lyric.

Throughout the Depression years and up to and including World War 2, the blues were recorded extensively. This was nowhere more apparent than in Chicago where the country blues was most subject to the imposition of urban qualities. Although considerable Southern influences can still be discerned in the blues of Chicago in the 1930s, there was now a tougher and more exhilarating quality to the songs being sung. The blues were becoming more extrovert and street-wise. Heading the trend-setters were Big Bill Broonzy and Leroy Carr, but they were far from being alone.

Big Bill Broonzy (1893–1958) emerged in the 1930s as one of the prime movers in blues recording in Chicago. He stamped his authority not only on titles recorded under his own name but also on record dates in the names of others. Jazz Gillum, Washboard Sam, Roosevelt Sykes and Lil Green all had the Broonzy stamp on them by way of either his guitar work or by performing his compositions. Broonzy was one of the most original and inventive blues singers as well as being one of the most influential. The strutting quality of his recordings helped further the music along the road which led to the rhythm-and-blues boom of the 1940s, as demonstrated by the almost vaudevillean declarations on *Keep Your Hands Off Her*, where he is accompanied by pianist Black Bob, and *All By Myself* on which the singer is driven along by the piano of Memphis Slim.

Leroy Carr (1905–35) sang in a bitter-sweet manner accompanied

Big Bill Broonzy – prime mover; (*clockwise from top left*) Blind Lemon
Jefferson, Leroy Carr, Doc Clayton, Lightnin' Hopkins, Brownie McGhee,
Roosevelt Sykes.

by his own rolling piano and the guitar of his partner, Scrapper
Blackwell. His were perhaps the most influential blues recordings
made by any individual artist in the 1930s. He composed many songs
which are still performed today: *How Long, How Long Blues,
Midnight Hour Blues, Hurry Down Sunshine* and *Blues Before Sunrise*.

Lonnie Johnson remained as important and influential in the
1930s as he had been in the 1920s, recording many of his finest blues
including *Jersey Belle Blues*, with Joshua Altheimer (p), and *Lapleg-
ged Drunk Again*. He also recorded many superb guitar solos among
them *Got The Blues For West End*. Johnson's vocalising, as heard on
Blue Ghost Blues had become even smoother than in the 1920s with
many of his blues being treated almost as straight ballads.

73

Sonny Boy Williamson (1914–48) had a unique vocal style due mainly to a speech impediment. A much-imitated harmonica player, he developed the technique of alternating voice and instrument until they blended into a continuous wailing line. A similar singing and playing style was used by Aleck 'Rice' Miller (1899–1965) who also used the name Sonny Boy Williamson. This singer found unusual devotees among young British rock singers of the early 1960s with whom he played on European tours.

Hudson 'Tampa Red' Whittaker (c.1902–81) was one of the more important country blues singers, despite being overtaken by harder, more driving bluesmen. A light-voiced singer, he was a master of the bottle-neck style of guitar playing and recorded with Georgia Tom Dorsey whom he met when both were with Ma Rainey's travelling show.

Peetie Wheatstraw (1902–41), 'The Devil's Son-in-Law', had an indistinct voice and was at his best with medium to slow blues, and on his recording of *All Night Long Blues* are good examples of his habit of linking phrases through barely audible use of the words 'well, well'. This vocal effect is also noticable in the work of Merline Johnson, 'The Yas-Yas Girl'.

Jazz Gillum sang in a low-pitched, detached voice, although his blues displayed a measure of originality. Tommy McLennan had a harsh and rather flat voice which he used with ferocious intensity. His most popular record was *Bottle It Up And Go*. Washboard Sam sang blues songs of considerable interest, while pianists Big Maceo Merriweather and Roosevelt Sykes were also fine singers and recorded many excellent titles.

Other blues singers of merit include Kokomo Arnold whose assured and confident style is demonstrated on *Milk Cow Blues* and *Original Kokomo Blues*. Brownie McGhee's warm and rhythmic voice was used to good effect on many records and he was, of course, well known for his long-lasting partnership with Sonny Terry which kept him in the public eye until recent times. Bumble Bee Slim and Sunnyland Slim were always personable singers and easy to listen to.

A blues singer who never attained widespread popularity in his lifetime but who proved to be of great influence on later generations of singers was Robert Johnson (c.1912–38) of Mississippi. His brooding, intense singing of the blues, perfectly illuminated by his distinctive and much admired guitar work, have made him a figure of much latterday interest and scholarship.

Big Joe Williams, also hailing from the Mississippi Delta, was an impressively inventive performer both as singer and guitarist. *Peach Orchard Mama, I'm Getting Wild About Her* and *Crawlin' King Snake* were among his better-known songs. An occasional element of country hokum is apparent in some of Big Joe's accompaniment and this has tended to obscure the solid blues core of his work.

On the distaff side, Memphis Minnie (1897–1973) was similar to Broonzy. She recorded many superb titles, among the best being *Good Morning Blues* which she sings in a lean, mocking manner urged on by her own driving guitar. It is typical of the many rewarding sides she recorded in the 1930s and on into the 1940s. Her career was centred mainly in small, local clubs. Langston Hughes, recalling seeing her in such a place, singing and playing guitar while perched atop a refrigerator, remarked that she had a voice which represented coloured America.

Among the innumerable blues and barrelhouse performers reached by those eager record company executives were Speckled Red, as approximate in his singing as he was in his piano playing; Walter Davis, who sang with a flat, unemotional voice; Big Boy Crudup, an original blues composer and good singer; Curtis Jones who was typically pleasant to hear if undistinguished in performance; and Peter 'Doc' Clayton who attracted attention as much through the content of his lyrics as for any other reason: 'I know blues singers don't go to Heaven because Gabriel bawls them out'.

The contrast between the work and the status of the country blues singer, even those who became urbanised in the 1930s, and other black entertainers such as those in Harlem, was striking. Even more contrasting was the reception given to those black artists who travelled to Europe between the wars. Many were women, some had played the Cotton Club, most had worked in one or another Harlem nightspot.

Although only a few were out-and-out jazz performers they

developed a delicate, jazz-inflected style of vocalising which entranced and delighted the after-hours set in Europe's capitals. These audiences often included kings and queens, princes, titled aristocracy, society hostesses, and millionaires. It was even swankier than the Harlem scene but with one major difference. European night-life welcomed these performers into its midst with little apparent regard for their colour. They mingled with the rich and famous, became the darlings of the 'gay young things', of high society, the 'in' crowd – whilst back home in America their contemporaries still struggled for recognition and still had to use the back entrances to those clubs which bore their names in lights over the marquee.

In the heady days of the 1920s and on into the doom-laden 1930s these ladies could do no wrong (although one of them would later spend a horrifying spell in a Nazi concentration camp). In Paris, Berlin and London, they were the queens of the ebony night.

One who began her career at the Cotton Club was Adelaide Hall (1909–) who was destined for immortality from the moment of her almost accidental involvement with the Duke Ellington Orchestra's version of *Creole Love Call*. When Duke heard her wordless vocalising to the band's instrumental performance he took her into the recording studios and they made the definitive version of this song. This was in 1927 and in 1975 she was still recording, now in England which has long been her home, and still favouring Ellington's music. Indeed, for Ellington memorial concerts in England in 1984 and 1985, her appearance was seemingly *de rigueur*. She has a light, flexible voice and her sense of style is perfectly balanced with a degree of sophistication and warmth rarely encountered in popular singing. She has the ability to project the feeling of a lyric with great finesse. Not always at ease with a fast tempo, her forte is the slow, meaningful ballad which she invariably portrays with rare skill and sensitivity.

Valaida Snow (1900–56) was a remarkably gifted artist. In addition to singing and dancing she played trumpet to a standard which, had she been a man, would have assured her of greater fame. She worked in China and most countries in Europe. She was in Denmark when World War 2 began and when the Germans invaded her American nationality weighed little against the fact that she was black. She was imprisoned in a concentration camp where she

Adelaide Hall – skill and sensitivity.

suffered severe hardship, humiliation and beatings. After a year and a half she was repatriated to America and resumed her career but was ever afterwards scarred in mind and body.

Una Mae Carlisle (1918–56) was discovered by Fats Waller and worked with him before going solo. A fine example of the Carlisle-Waller partnership can be heard on *I Can't Give You Anything But Love* recorded in 1939 where Waller's sense of fun and Carlisle's husky, intimate voice contrast effectively. She was highly successful in England, Germany and France where she worked at 'Boeuf sur le Toit' in Paris. In 1941 she recorded with the John Kirby Orchestra and good examples of her delayed phrasing and warm sensual voice are heard on *You Mean So Much To Me, It Ain't Like That* and *Oh! I'm Evil.*

Even further afield than Europe went Midge Williams. She toured extensively in the Far East, working in both China and Japan where she recorded Japanese-language versions of *Dinah* and *Lazybones*. Her American work included a spell with Louis Armstrong's Orchestra and she also recorded with her own Jazz Jesters, effectively a reconstituted John Kirby band, with whom she made a jaunty, if unexceptional version of *Rosie The Redskin*. On record, Midge's vocal charm rarely came through due perhaps to the poor quality of her material. Sometimes she tried to imbue her work with a plaintive air but usually succeeded only in sounding somewhat mournful as on *Where In The World* and *Don't Wake Up My Heart*.

Another stylish singer was Nina Mae McKinney who is primarily remembered as a dancer. An extremely beautiful young woman, she made many films both in Hollywood and England, including playing opposite Paul Robeson in *Sanders Of The River* (1935). Elisabeth Welch also worked extensively in films and theatres in England. Her West End stage performances included Cole Porter's 'Nymph Errant' from which came *Solomon*, one of her most successful recordings. Among her co-stars in films was Paul Robeson. In 1985, Elisabeth Welch was still starring in London stage shows and displaying all her old panache.

Among those artists who stayed behind and enjoyed some success in Harlem was Monette Moore. Well known in vaudeville and to the record-buying public in the 1920s, she had a limited range and sang with a pronounced but controlled vibrato. In the 1940s Monette moved to the West Coast where she worked in clubs and shows before returning east and into semi-retirement. She attempted a comeback in the 1960s but died at an engagement at Disneyland.

Ada Brown made very few recordings but proved her considerable abilities as a blues singer in Harlem nightspots and in London in the 1930s. She appeared in the film *Stormy Weather* where her performance of *That Ain't Right*, a song written by Nat 'King' Cole, was quite superb. Inez Cavanaugh and Thelma Carpenter were two other pleasant if unexceptional singers in the same vein. Cavanaugh achieved localised fame in Europe, while Carpenter enjoyed some success with the Count Basie Orchestra in the 1940s and with whom she recorded *I Didn't Know About You*. She also appeared in the 1985 film, *The Cotton Club*.

In New York, the real Cotton Club provided the base for another band after Ellington's departure in 1931. This was the band led by Cab Calloway.

Calloway (1907–) was born in Rochester, NY, and during the 1920s worked as drummer, singer and emcee in various shows and clubs, especially around Chicago where the family had moved. For a time he worked with his sister Blanche and then joined the Missourians, a band which eventually metamorphosed into the Cab Calloway Orchestra. The Cotton Club residency was an important factor in Calloway's rise to national fame but so too were his songs, his manner of dress, his catchphrase, and his vocal eccentricities. Such things tended to obscure the fact that the Calloway band was home to some of the finest jazz musicians of the era, especially in the late-1930s.

Calloway's songs included several enormous hits and this, allied to his outrageous personal appearance assured him of a prominent place in the public eye. His knee-length drape jacket, the voluminous trousers, floor-trailing watch chain and huge, wide-brimmed hat provided a model for the thousands who followed his sartorial example. His catchphrase, 'Hi-De-Hi', lives on, albeit often in the least likeliest of places and where its originator possibly remains unknown.

As a singer Calloway's real qualities emerge in the relatively few non-nonsense songs he performed. Quite clearly, the record companies had a beady eye on their cash registers and insisted on a high output of the comic routines, yet even these have their moments. Apart from anything else, Calloway regularly sneaked in songs about drugs, booze and sex but with lyrics couched in euphemisms which slipped unnoticed past the executives. Even his biggest hit, *Minnie The Moocher*, is a drugs song, as is *Kicking The Gong Around*, another great success.

Geechy Joe, which was recorded both commercially and for the 1943 movie *Stormy Weather*, in which he appeared, is delivered in a powerful fashion with the singer's voice taking on almost cantorial overtones towards the end. Another song which reflected Calloway's religious upbringing comes in *Stormy Weather*. This is an excellent, if over-solemn version of *Sunday In Savannah*. Then there is *The Jumpin' Jive*, with its mixture of straight and scat lyrics, and an engaging duet with Lena Horne, another Cotton Club alumnus, on a somewhat overblown version of *I Can't Give You Anything But Love, Baby*.

On the occasions when he moved into· blues material, Calloway showed that if he chose he could interpret them well, albeit with a highly personal flavour. It was in his early 1930s recordings, however, that Calloway performed his most typical songs.

Hugely prolific at this time, the examples from 1931 alone are numerous. *Minnie The Moocher* came in March and contains in its lyrics not only references to cocaine and opium addiction but most of Calloway's nonsense phrases including, hi-de-hi, ho-de-ho, which are called by him and echoed by the band in chorus. This song had a new lease of life when Calloway sang it in the 1980 film *The Blues Brothers* although most money was made in the 1940s by Danny Kaye who sang it in his act which then strongly reflected Calloway's influence. *Kicking The Gong Around* from October 1931 picks up the story of Minnie the Moocher and her boyfriend Smokey and quite clearly, whatever they might be doing to the euphemistic gong, their habit has not been kicked. On the same session, Calloway stretched the naivety of the record company bosses still further with

Cab Calloway – timelessly outrageous.

Triggeration, a Harold Arlen-Ted Koehler song about sexual prowess. Even a comic song like *I'll Be Glad When You're Dead, You Rascal You!* takes on an unexpected eroticism with Calloway's interpretation while *Six Or Seven Times*, a Fats Waller composition, leaves the listener in no doubt what is wanted that number of times.

Calloway's career as a bandleader continued into the 1940s when he largely built on his established repertoire with songs such as *The Jumpin' Jive*, the lyrics of which suited the new generation of hep cats and zoot-suited jive brothers.

In later years, he developed a career as a movie actor which brought him to the delighted attention of a new audience in the 1970s. The outrageousness in dress, performance and in the lyrics he sang, suited new concepts in popular music. Or, rather, he proved that there really was nothing new under the sun and that if he had occasionally been unfashionable, he was essentially timeless in his appeal.

In 1985, when the film *The Cotton Club* reawakened interest in an era a half-century ago, Calloway was 'discovered' all over again, this time at the age of 78.

Although Cab Calloway's importance in jazz is obscured for some observers by his delight in performing comic material, the talents of Thomas 'Fats' Waller (1904–43) rarely suffer the same fate, even though he had a similar penchant. Nevertheless, there is a tendency for some critics to praise Fats' non-vocal work while politely

Fats Waller.

82

ignoring his songs. This is an unnecessary evasion for even at his most flamboyant, whether singing or verbally exhorting himself and his fellow musicians on to greater things, Fats had an unerring sense of timing and his rhythmic interpretation is always superb, even on such seemingly unpromising material as *Serenade For A Wealthy Widow, Eep, Ipe, Wanna Piece Of Pie, Patty Cake, Patty Cake, Your Feet's Too Big* and *All That Meat And No Potatoes.*

Forty years after his death, Fats Waller has retained a surprisingly wide and appreciative audience outside the jazz world. The most popular of his songs are excellent examples of how a singer of special talent can imbue some parts of his repertoire with qualities which demand a wider public. *Ain't Misbehavin', Honeysuckle Rose, I'm Crazy 'Bout My Baby, I've Got A Feeling I'm Falling* and *Black And Blue* – all his own compositions (several with lyrics by his major collaborator Andy Razaf) – have that quality of timelessness both intrinsically and in performance which transcend artificial boundaries. Despite having been performed by numerous other singers no other artist has brought to these songs Fats' blend of earthy good humour, infectious enthusiasm, and effortless swing.

Frequently hard-up, Fats resorted to selling songs outright for a few dollars. Reputedly many popular standards, although bearing the names of others, came originally from him.

When performing the songs of others, Fats loved to insert jokey embellishments, probably out of a desire to break away from the rigidity imposed by a formal lyric which was often stultifyingly banal.

The blues were not especially important to Fats as a piano player and even less so as a singer. Yet, in much of his recorded work, especially towards the end of his short life, appear many elements which are far removed from the light-heartedness of *My Very Good Friend The Milkman*. The spirituals he recorded on organ in London in 1938 and his extended composition *The London Suite* from 1939, all display the usually well-hidden serious side of his nature. These are all non-vocal, however, but, when needed, Fats could sing with deep feeling even if the material on which he did so was sometimes unworthy.

A man of monumental proportions and gargantuan appetites, Fats' powerful stride piano-playing contrasted interestingly with his voice which was surprisingly light for such a big man.

Earl Hines' tune *Rosetta* is a good example of Fats playing and singing a better-than-average song with affectionate seriousness. *Two Sleepy People* is also taken seriously, although Fats contrives to avoid the potentially dangerous sentimentality of the lyric.

In 1943 Fats Waller was taken ill while aboard the 'Santa Fe Chief' and when the train pulled into Kansas City he was dead; he was thirty-nine.

Billy Banks was a product of the black vaudeville circuits and sang for a while with Noble Sissle's band. An infectious performer, he is remembered best for his Rhythmmakers recordings. The ones in this series are among the hottest examples of Chicago jazz ever recorded.

Putney Dandridge, who accompanied Bill 'Bojangles' Robinson for a while, and Bob Howard, one of the few black entertainers to have a sponsored radio show in the 1930s, were also well served by the bands with whom they recorded and were frequently lifted to heights they would not have achieved if left to their own devices.

Blanche Calloway, Cab's older sister, worked at New York's Ciro Club in the mid-1920s before touring extensively with occasional residencies in Chicago and Philadelphia where she fronted the Andy Kirk band. A happy, extrovert performer, she led a band through the 1930s, but went broke in 1938 and thereafter worked as a solo singer. Later, she managed the career of singer Ruth Brown.

Blanche's singing voice was undistinguished, occasionally a trifle forced in the higher register, and as a performer really qualified for the wider descriptive term, 'entertainer'. Her earlier recordings, which include *Lazy Woman's Blues* and *Lonesome Lovesick Blues*, recorded in 1925 with Louis Armstrong's cornet accompaniment, show her in a very different light to the performances which came later. By the time of her 1930s recordings with her Joy Boys the blues had given way to more commercially acceptable material even though she usually managed to swing.

Another extrovert artist was Lillian Hardin who, although relatively undistinguished as a singer, deserves her place in jazz histories for other reasons. A fine pianist, she joined King Oliver's band in 1921 at the Royal Gardens in Chicago. When young Louis Armstrong joined Oliver, Lillian took notice of him first as a musician, then as a man. They were married and she was in-

84

strumental in redirecting and furthering Armstrong's career.

Lil's own career fluctuated, especially after she and Louis split up in 1931. During the 1930s, like Blanche Calloway, she led a good band which never attracted the attention it deserved, almost certainly because she was a woman in what most people still regarded as a man's world. As both bandleader and singer, Lil favoured the popular tunes of the day: *My Hi-De-Ho Man, Doin' The Suzy Q, It's Murder* and the like. One song she herself wrote, *Just For A Thrill*, had a new lease of life in the 1950s when recorded by Ray Charles.

Lil Hardin died while performing at a Chicago concert honouring Louis Armstrong who had died a few weeks earlier.

Blanche Calloway and Lil Hardin Armstrong were not alone in failing to find commercial success in the 1930s. Mildred Bailey, a singer of extraordinary merit also found difficulty in gaining general public acceptance.

The singing of Mildred Bailey (1907–51) proved timeless, a quality which can be seen in the work of all the best jazz singers. For more than two decades she straddled the gap between pure jazz and its more commercial cousin, swing music, successfully retaining the respect of musicians and fellow vocalists with her innate sense of style and good taste.

In her early teens, she began working as a song demonstrator, later touring the West Coast in revue and by the time she was 18 was holding down a spot in one of Hollywood's plushier speakeasies. There, she interspersed the popular songs of the day with blues and slightly risqué vaudeville numbers.

After working on radio for a time she submitted a demonstration disc to Paul Whiteman and from 1929 to 1933 became one of the brightest lights of his frequently ponderous organisation. While with Whiteman she worked alongside such notable artists as Bing Crosby, and her brother Al Rinker (who had called on her when they first ventured into show-business), saxophonist Frank Trumbauer and xylophonist Red Norvo. During this period she made a number of records with both the Whiteman Orchestra and the up-and-coming Casa Loma Orchestra.

Leaving Whiteman's band, she married Red Norvo in 1933 and began making a long series of records with various small groups in whose ranks were many top-flight jazzmen of the day. In musical surroundings such as these Mildred Bailey truly excelled. She had a way of riding a melody which gave even the most trite of lyrics a certain dignity. Her exquisite delivery, coupled with a fragile tenderness and a sparingly-used subtle vibrato made her unique. She displayed an extraordinary ability to swing without ever discarding the original melody.

In December 1935, Mildred took part in a session in New York supervised by John Hammond, and originally recorded specifically for issue in Britain. She is given particularly splendid support by three great jazz soloists. Incisive playing by Bunny Berigan (tp), the insinuating alto saxophone of Johnny Hodges, and an immaculate yet surprisingly downhome performance by Teddy Wilson (p), all contribute to this near-perfect recording session. The four tracks recorded on this date, two standards and two blues which show Mildred at her very best, are untypical of her general output as they were a deliberate attempt by Hammond to create a set of pure jazz performances directly for the British jazz audience. The titles recorded were *Willow Tree, Honeysuckle Rose, Squeeze Me* and *Down Hearted Blues*. Her blues interpretations hark back to an earlier era and her delight at singing them is clearly evident in her easy and relaxed performances. Here, as elsewhere in her career, she demonstrated her ability to pick up every nuance of a melody or lyric and make of it something that had not been there before.

Mildred was best known for her rendition of Hoagy Carmichael's *Rockin' Chair*, which she recorded on numerous occasions, thus gaining the soubriquet 'The Rocking Chair Lady'. She was never better, however, than on a version recorded on 23 September 1937 where she was superbly backed by Red Norvo and his Orchestra.

During the late 1930s she recorded many tasteful performances. Particularly fine examples of her easy style are *Heaven Help This Heart Of Mine, Thanks For The Memory, I've Got My Love To Keep Me Warm, Don't Be That Way, Bob White* and a most sensitive version of Ellington's *I Let A Song Go Out Of My Heart*.

Possessor of only a small, plaintive, yet sweet and pure voice, Mildred Bailey was big in every other way: in temperament, especially in heart, and also in physique. Her size troubled her but she had a sense of humour about most things, even her bulk, as was demonstrated during an evening at the home of John Hammond's

86

(*Clockwise from top left*) Maxine Sullivan – highly musical; Helen Humes – bell-like optimism; Mildred Bailey – sweet and pure; Lee Wiley – low-key sensuality.

parents where she was attending a recital by Benny Goodman. The chair occupied by one of the host's society friends was accidentally knocked over by bandleader Charlie Barnet. As the lady went crashing to the floor, Mildred looked down at the fragile chair she was sitting on and asked the momentarily silent gathering, 'How'm I doin'?'

Among the very finest of jazz singers, Mildred Bailey's chronically poor health finally failed completely and she died when only forty-four.

Another fine white singer of the period was Lee Wiley (1915–75) who was, like Mildred Bailey, part-American Indian. She too worked extensively with jazz musicians, particularly those associated with Chicago. In the late 1930s and on through the 1940s she made many fine recordings, even if, oftentimes, she was hampered by having to perform inferior material. Her voice, although small, held a wistful charm coupled with a low-key sensuality which concentrated attention upon every word of the lyric. A fine example is the thoughtful way in which she phrases the introductory verse of *I've Got A Crush On You* on her 1939 recording with an augmented Eddie Condon gang, and then follows with an exquisitely sung chorus. Phrasing, however, was only part of the reason for the esteem in which she was held by her fellow musicians. There was a warmth of tone, an intimacy, about her voice which has since been seldom equalled. In all her work, Lee Wiley appeared always to be singing directly to the individual listener. On *I've Got A Crush On You* she has the added benefit of Fats Waller, in brilliant form on piano, and Bud Freeman, whose tenor saxophone playing always complemented Lee's haunting style and displayed an obvious rapport with her interpretation of the melody line.

1939 and 1940 were significant years in her career for this was when she made her best records. Especially notable from these years are *Sweet And Lowdown*, *My One And Only* and *How Long Has This Been Going On?* which offer perfect examples of Lee's lazy beat.

On some of the 1940 sessions she is joined by Bunny Berigan whose fine support lends an easy swing to *Let's Do It* and *Hot House*. On *Baby's Awake Now* and *A Little Birdie Told Me So*, a loose-knit group features Max Kaminsky (tp), Freeman, and the always supportive piano, bass and drums team of Joe Bushkin, Sid Weiss and George Wettling. Also of particular note is *You Took Advantage Of Me* where the same musicians weave a beautiful backcloth behind Lee's distinctive singing.

Although in good voice throughout the 1940s, the backing groups used on her recordings rarely recaptured the sparkling rapport which was so evident in the 1939–40 sessions. Nevertheless, some good records were made, in particular *Stormy Weather* and *Down With Love* from 1945, on which a group led by Eddie Condon includes beautiful trumpet playing by Billy Butterfield.

In the 1950s and 1960s Lee recorded occasionally, and in 1963 a semi-biographical film of her life was made for TV. One of her last public performances was at the 1972 New York Jazz Festival.

Although rapturously received, her voice had only a hint of its former delicate glory.

A contemporary of Lee Wiley and Mildred Bailey was not only the best of her era but remains the best a quarter-century after her death. She is Billie Holiday who, like Louis Armstrong before her, changed forever the style and sound of American popular music.

Billie Holiday (c.1915–59) was a true original – more than that, she was unique. Although she often spoke of being influenced by Louis Armstrong and Bessie Smith such influences are felt rather than heard. In Billie's singing there is a more direct relationship with the Ethel Waters lineage, although this too is only super-ficial.

Certainly, when John Hammond first heard her, singing at Monette Moore's club in New York, he knew at once that this was a major talent.

Billie's assured style, with its casual, off-hand phrasing, was intuitive and was evident from the start, although her first record-ings, organised by Hammond, do not wholly confirm this. *Your Mother's Son-In-Law* and *Riffin' The Scotch*, recorded in November and December 1933, are pleasant but unexceptional performances. This was the last occasion on which anyone could be noncommittal about her.

Billie rarely sang the blues, but a strong blues feeling permeated everything she sang, be it a superior ballad or a trite novelty song. Curiously enough, however, two of her best-remembered songs were blues: *Billie's Blues* and *Fine And Mellow*, on which she acquits herself as well as any thoroughgoing blues singer. Her astonishingly subtle rephrasing of a melody line and her beautifully timed delivery came to the fore in 1935 when she began a series of recordings with pick-up groups led by pianist Teddy Wilson. These groups featured some of the greatest jazz soloists of the period, culled mainly from the big bands of Count Basie, Duke Ellington and Cab Calloway, and from the small groups who could be heard along New York's 52nd Street. These records are among the most startlingly beautiful in the history of jazz. In the history of jazz singing they are unequalled.

I Wished On The Moon, from the first of these sessions, signalled a level of artistry which rarely fell below excellent. Billie's relaxed phrasing emphasises the lyrics quite differently to the way intended by the composer. On *What A Little Moonlight Can Do* her projection of the first 'Ooh, ooh, ooh' is totally instrumental in form and her performance lifts this dire song with its unimpressive melody and lyric of monumental banality to unimaginable heights. *Miss Brown To You*, with its incongruous lyrics is marvellously sung by Billie, who is backed by some superb clarinet and piano from Benny Goodman and Teddy Wilson. In 1936, accompanied by a small band which included Johnny Hodges on alto saxophone, Billie recorded the definitive version of *I Cried For You*. Later the same year she recorded an impeccable *A Fine Romance* with Bunny Berigan and Irving Fazola (cl).

Never a scat singer, Billie never needed to alter lyrics, her originality lay entirely in her restructuring of the notes within the natural harmonies of a song. A good example of this technique is her 1936 version of *I Can't Give You Anything But Love*.

A session on 25 January 1937 was one of the most significant dates in jazz history for it was then that Billie first recorded with her *alter ego*, tenor saxophonist Lester Young. Together, they consolidated their individual greatness and produced recordings of unsurpassed beauty. Lester's introduction on *Mean To Me* fits Billie's mood superbly. Their spirits are totally at one. Lester's improvisation on *When You're Smiling* is one of the best-known jazz solos ever recorded and its qualities never cease to amaze. Billie's vocal is equal to the occasion, as is Buck Clayton's muted trumpet work. The lesser known *Foolin' Myself* is also a magnificent example of the immaculate interaction between Billie and Lester. The combination of these two artists cannot simply be considered as vocal with instrumental obbligato; theirs is an equal partnership, a duet of absolute perfection. This quality is unmistakable in yet another collaboration which touches genius: *This Year's Kisses*, where Billie endows a trivial lyric with profound beauty. Lester Young is in tender mood, faultlessly cushioning the vocal. The personal relationship between Billie and Lester (Lady Day and Prez, as they

90

Billie Holiday – matchless.

called one another) was apparently platonic but after listening to their work together no one can doubt that theirs was a friendship of uncommon depth, respect and affection.

The startling differences in style between Billie and her contemporaries can be heard in recordings of *My Last Affair* made by Billie and her two closest artistic rivals in the 1930s, Mildred Bailey and Helen Humes. All recorded excellent versions of this song but the difference in emphasis is remarkable. Helen sings it with beautiful directness and power; Mildred with a lilting, enchanting tone and crystalline diction. Billie has neither Helen's strength nor Mildred's tone, but hers is the definitive jazz performance – expressive and intense with an emotional penetration which the others cannot equal.

In 1939 Billie recorded *Strange Fruit* for Milt Gabler's Commodore label. This stark and chilling song marks a change in emphasis in Billie's stylistic progress. It also made her a star. For the first time the public at large began to hear of her and she duly took note of what had caused this change.

Working on 52nd Street during this period, Billie began to listen to the night club performer Mabel Mercer, an artist with a remarkable ability to dramatise a lyric through exceptional subtlety of phrasing. Mercer's influence is heard increasingly in Billie's performances as she adopted a more positive attitude towards the lyrics of her material. The casually-made masterpieces of the 1930s were overtaken by the dramatic performances of the 1940s. On records at least, the musicians she worked with became merely accompaniment, with none of the involvement displayed by Prez, Teddy and Buck and the others. But the voice remained superb.

In 1944 Billie began recording for Decca and, as with many other singers who came under this particular banner, the jazz content diminished. Among other Decca singers of the period were Bing Crosby and Ella Fitzgerald, both of whom were subjected to all kinds of novelty accompaniment.

Nevertheless, none of these three appeared averse to this policy, seemingly content with their commercial success. Indeed, Billie was pleased to be singing in front of string sections and heavenly choirs; the record-buying public was also happy and sales rose. Her voice remained at its best while her phrasing displayed even more subtlety.

92

Such singers as the young Peggy Lee and Frank Sinatra paid increasing attention to Billie's phrasing during this period. In an interview in *Ebony* magazine in July, 1958, Sinatra commented: 'But it is Billie Holiday whom I first heard on 52nd Street in the early 1930s, who was and still remains the greatest single musical influence on me. It has been a warm and wonderful influence and I am proud to acknowledge it. Lady Day is unquestionably the most important influence on American popular singing in the last twenty years. With a few exceptions every major pop singer in the US during her generation has been touched in some way by her genius.'

The 1950s brought a diminution of Billie's qualities of greatness. Due to her personal problems, which included drink, drugs and emotional distress caused by the men in her life, and which were acute at this time, her pitching became suspect, her tone flattened out and the zest was now clearly absent. When she sang badly she was tragic, but even at this time, when she hit form she was in many ways equal to her own classic period. As singer Carmen McRae observed, one night she might sound as if her career were over, then 'the next night she sings her ass off, pardon my expression'.

Billie's vocal range was narrower now and her vibrato had coarsened but her artistry was still intact. This is clearly demonstrated in her poignant reading of *My Man* and a shattering *He's Funny That Way* recorded in 1952. *My Man* again came in for a similarly moving treatment at a 1954 Carnegie Hall concert with Count Basie. This was on a bill which also featured a melancholy Lester Young performing *Pennies From Heaven*.

In 1955, after a very successful concert at the Hollywood Bowl, Billie recorded two albums, 'Music for Torching' and 'Velvet Mood' which show her at her most tender on ballads while the livelier songs are sung with wry humour. Backing her are Harry Edison (tp), Benny Carter (as), Jimmy Rowles (p), John Simmons (b) and Larry Bunker (d). Their sympathetic accompaniment is almost equal to that of the Teddy Wilson sessions of the 1930s. The same can be said of the album 'Songs for Distingué Lovers' on which Billie's rendition of *One For My Baby* is superlative.

Close to the end of her life, Billie recorded an album, 'Lady in Satin', with backing from the Ray Ellis Strings. Here the ravages of her tragic life can be clearly heard. Her voice, broken now, has a harsh edge to it and her range is minimal. Yet her phrasing remains unimpaired and there is an emotional depth to her voice which makes even this flawed album a remarkably moving experience.

'Lady in Satin' was made in March 1959 and within a few months Billie was hospitalised when her health finally gave way. Harrassed as she had been for decades by the forces of law and order, she was subjected to a last indignity when she was arrested for possession of narcotics while lying terminally ill in a ward at New York's Metropolitan Hospital. Billie never had to face the charges, however, because she never left the hospital. She died there on 17 July 1959.

Just as New Orleans and Chicago proved useful as focal points for musical events in earlier decades, so another American city served this purpose in the 1930s – Kansas City.

Like those other two centres, Kansas City was a major transportation confluence, like them it enjoyed an 'anything goes' policy – promoted by Mayor Tom Pendergast – which led to the flourishing of crime, prostitution and all kinds of entertainment. Now beginning to wear its association with the lowlife with a combination of resignation and pride, jazz too flourished in Kansas City. This was where Lester Young first attracted wider attention with the locally-based band of Count Basie (which had grown out of Bennie Moten's band and Walter Page's Blue Devils). KC was also an important centre for a special kind of singer – the so-called 'blues shouters', a term which obscures the extraordinary merits of a number of very gifted performers.

Although he reached fame with the greatest of the KC bands, Jimmy Rushing (1903–72) hailed from Oklahoma City. Taught violin and piano privately, he also studied music at a local high school and soon began singing, mainly locally but occasionally moving as far afield as California where he worked for a while with Jelly Roll Morton.

In 1927 Jimmy joined Walter Page's Blue Devils, a band which was home to many later giants of jazz. He recorded with the band, a song entitled *Blue Devil Blues*, and then, in 1929, was one among numerous Blue Devils who moved over to the Bennie Moten band.

Jimmy's voice was a high tenor and possessed a slightly nasal quality which proved surprisingly attractive. Also surprising was the manner in which his voice carries over the roar of a powerful band and, as writer Ralph Ellison (who grew up in Oklahoma City) recalled, Jimmy could be heard several blocks from Slaughter's Hall where he sometimes worked. The high pitch and the nasal sound gave Jimmy's voice a keening, plaintive quality which brought to the blues a romantic lyricism few other blues singers ever achieved. Not that Jimmy ever considered himself to be a blues singer. Rightly so, for few of his performances were purely blues, rather he tinged everything he sang, from ballads to up-tempo swingers, with the qualities of the blues.

With Moten he recorded excellent versions of *New Orleans, As Long As I Love You* and a rousing *That Too, Do,* which was a forerunner of his later hit, *Good Morning Blues.* When the Moten band metamorphosed into the Count Basie band, Jimmy Rushing proved to be one of its greatest assets. By no means could he be regarded as merely a singer who came on, sang a song or two, and went off again. More than any other big band singer, Jimmy Rushing was a fully-fledged member of the band, his voice being an important instrumental addition to the ensemble.

With Basie, Jimmy had a string of successes: *Boo Hoo, Exactly Like You, Boogie Woogie, Evenin'* and *Good Morning Blues* (which he co-composed) were among the earliest. On this last song and on *Don't You Miss Your Baby,* which is another fine example, Buck Clayton's muted trumpet provides an excellent foil to Jimmy's singing. Indeed, the mutual empathy obviously felt by the entire Basie crew on all its recordings of this period is especially noticable when Jimmy is singing.

By now, Jimmy's youthful rotundity had given way to positively barrel-like proportions and he was tagged with the name 'Mr Five by Five' but he remained a snappy dresser and a remarkably agile mover as his occasional on-stage dance steps testified.

Later recordings with Basie include a superbly relaxed *I Left My Baby* and an excellent *Goin' To Chicago* (a co-composition with Basie), on which he is backed by Buck Clayton, *Take Me Back, Baby,* with Tab Smith (as) and Dickie Wells (tb) in fine form, and *Rusty Dusty Blues.*

No longer with Basie after 1950, Jimmy led a small group for a while before beginning, in 1952, a solo career which lasted through the next two decades. In the mid-1950s he made some of his best recordings backed by small groups which included Basie-ites Buddy Tate (ts), Walter Page (b) and Jo Jones (d) – *Boogie Woogie, See See Rider, Goin' To Chicago, How Long, How Long Blues* and *Sent For You Yesterday* – and clearly benefited from the improved facilities of the new microgroove recordings. More than ever before, his clarity of diction was distinctively and fully realised by the new recording techniques.

In 1955, Jimmy was in even better form on a session which again featured Tate, Page and Jones and the added (and considerable) talents of blues and boogie-woogie pianist Pete Johnson. This session produced definitive versions of *Good Morning Blues* and *Evenin'*, together with a sparkling *Rock And Roll*.

In the 1960s Jimmy toured and recorded extensively but only occasionally (as on his 1960 session with the Dave Brubeck Quartet) did he venture outside his familiar repertoire.

In 1969 Jimmy took an acting role in the movie, *The Learning Tree*, and continued working clubs as the new decade opened. Time was running out, however, both for the voice and the singer himself. Fortunately, the kind of thing that almost never happens with jazz artists happened with Jimmy Rushing. Just before his death in 1972, he was persuaded by record producer Don Schlitten to make an album arranged by pianist-composer-singer Dave Frishberg. This time the endless performances of *Exactly Like You, Goin' To Chicago, 'Deed I Do* and the like were abandoned in favour of a selection of popular songs which, while richly varied, were all superbly suited to Jimmy's rugged lyricism. True, the rusty voice was now noticably flaking, but the emotional depth remained, as did the unflagging swing. The accompanying musicians excel themselves: ex-Ellingtonian Ray Nance plays trumpet and, on an exquisite *When I Grow Too Old To Dream*, opens the proceedings with an out-of-tempo violin solo that prepares the listener for a tearful performance. But then the rhythm section, and Jimmy, pick up the tempo and swing home without ever losing that initial poignancy.

Apart from his arrangements, Frishberg's contributions to the album are exemplary. In particular, he and Jimmy duet on two songs

Jimmy Rushing – inimitable.

and in this setting, piano and voice only, Jimmy's ability to wring from a lyric everything the writer put there, and then some, is marvellously defined. These two songs are *I Surrender Dear* and *More Than You Know*. Jimmy never was one for embellishing lyrics with unnecessary touches and here his direct, deceptively simple phrasing provides examples for any singer to follow. Writing of Jimmy's touch on songs like this, Ralph Ellison, who as a child lay in his bed in Oklahoma City listening to Jimmy's voice carrying through the night, commented that the singer brought to ballads 'a sincerity and a feeling for dramatising the lyrics in the musical phrase which charged the banal lines with the mysterious potentiality of meaning which haunts the blues'.

Jimmy Rushing was an extraordinary singer, unmistakable, never imitated, a unique original. The closing phrase of *Jimmy's Blues*, one which he regularly tagged onto other songs, contained in its last line two declarations. The first was unnecessary because no one could ever doubt it; the second, sadly, was all too true:

> Anybody ask you
> Who was it sang this song
> Tell 'em little Jimmy Rushing
> He's been here and gone.

There was no room for a second-rate singer alongside Jimmy Rushing during the Basie band's heyday. Fortunately, the problem never arose. First, briefly, there was Billie Holiday. Then came Helen Humes.

Employed as replacement for Billie, it says much for Helen's personality and ability that she was quickly accepted by musicians and critics alike. Helen (1913–81) came from a close-knit middle-class family and enjoyed a happy and contented childhood in Louisville, Kentucky, where her interest in music was encouraged. Taught both trumpet and piano, she played and sang with the local Sunday School band which boasted such future jazz artists as Dickie Wells and Jonah Jones. As early as 1927, while she was still attending school, bluesman Sylvester Weaver recommended Helen to a recording agent and at his request she travelled with her mother to St Louis and there recorded four titles for OKeh. These included

Black Cat Blues and *Worried Woman's Blues*. Several months later she recorded eight more blues titles for OKeh, this time in New York, where she was accompanied by pianist James P. Johnson. It was not until 1937 that Count Basie heard Helen, offered her a job with the band, and was turned down flat. Apparently she did not think the money was good enough, but a little while later John Hammond heard her; he talked to Basie who repeated his offer. This time Helen accepted.

Between the recordings for OKeh and her first with Basie, Helen recorded with a pick-up band led by trumpeter Harry James. From the results Helen's principal objective seems to have been to produce the right sound even to the detriment of her pronunciation in some passages. This is typically a blues singer's approach, and is totally unlike Mildred Bailey's style, thus countering claims that Helen influenced her. In fact, from the time of the first recordings with Basie the reverse would seem to be true.

Generally, the choice of material given to Helen by Basie was somewhat uninspired – *My Heart Belongs To Daddy, It's Square But It Rocks, Moonlight Serenade*. Fortunately, however, some exceptional performances were notched up among the dross: *Dark Rapture, Someday, Sweetheart, Between The Devil And The Deep Blue Sea* and *If I Could Be With You One Hour Tonight*. If more care had been taken with Helen's career, and a more suitable repertoire compiled, it is conceivable that the stardom enjoyed by other artists with comparably long careers, notably Ella Fitzgerald and Lena Horne, could well have been hers. Certainly, Helen's was a special talent which remained largely unfulfilled, her career always lacking direction and purpose.

Helen stayed with the Count for four years, eventually quitting in 1941, by which time she had developed her own style. In 1944, after working various clubs, usually around New York, she headed for the West Coast where she appeared at a long string of nightspots. By now her repertoire had reverted to the blues and, with the upsurge of interest in rhythm-and-blues, numerous recording dates ensued. Her first session on the Coast, with the Bill Doggett Octet, resulted in a major hit, *Be-Baba-Leba*.

1947 saw Helen on a return visit to New York and some recording dates were supervised by John Hammond. These proved to be her most tasteful sessions of this period, very much in contrast to the strident rhythm-and-blues sides she had been cutting. With immaculate accompaniment from Buck Clayton, Teddy Wilson, Mundell Lowe (g) and others she made *They Raided The Joint, Jet Propelled Papa, Mad About You, Somebody Loves Me*, and a luscious *Blue And Sentimental* featuring the tenor saxophone of John Hardee. Other titles particularly worthy of attention are the blues ballads *I Just Refuse To Sing The Blues* and *Today I Sing The Blues*, both superbly performed by Helen as is an uptempo *Jumpin' On Sugar Hill*.

Back on the West Coast again, Helen was recorded at the 1950 'Blues Jubilee Concert' at the Shrine Auditorium in Los Angeles. Accompanied by the Roy Milton band she sang a song which became the Humes trademark, *Million Dollar Secret*. The success of this blues and the earlier *Be-Baba-Leba* directed her career along the lucrative but fickle rhythm-and-blues trail where gigs were plentiful if usually short term.

Unable to shake the rhythm-and-blues tag, Helen had difficulty in establishing herself as an album artist in the newly-arrived era of long-playing records. It was not until 1959 that her long overdue chance came but, despite some other fine recordings the late 1960s found her in enforced retirement through family illness. Then, in 1973, jazz writer and record producer Stanley Dance persuaded Helen out of retirement for an appearance with Count Basie at the Newport Jazz Festival. Although absent from the profession for six years and understandably nervous, Helen was a resounding success and her career blossomed.

She was now in her sixties but her voice still had the clear bell-like qualities of a young girl and the optimism of youth was very much in evidence. Communication was always Helen's forte and this quality too was apparent on her 1973 albums 'Helen Comes Back' and 'Sneakin' Around'. From them *Handy Man* and *Guess Who's In Town* offer exciting piano from Milt Buckner and delightfully laid-back vocalising by Helen, while on *Exactly Like You* and *Sometimes I'm Happy* she toys with and teases the melody, soaring and swooping over the Ben Webster-like tenor saxophone of Gerard Badini. Her personality is stamped indelibly on *I'm Confessin'* and the lesser-known but equally impressive *Every Now And Then*.

Whatever personal difficulties there might have been, in her recorded work Helen's happy and seemingly carefree personality is always in evidence. On the sleeve note of 'Sneakin' Around' she observed, 'When I sing I am the happiest person in the world, – and it shows.

Another singer of considerable note who worked in Kansas City in the 1930s was Joe Turner (1911–85). Joe earned a living as a singing bartender at various clubs until he eventually formed a long-lasting working partnership with pianist Pete Johnson. It was as a team that Joe and Pete went to New York in 1938 (at the urging of the ubiquitous John Hammond) and again the following year when the first venture proved to be of only limited success.

A powerful singer with a baritone voice which reflected his physical bulk (he stood six-two and tipped, if not upended, the scale at 250 pounds), Turner's driving, forceful style is almost entirely free of growls, vibrato or any of the other devices used by the classic blues singers and their descendants. This is not so much a quality unique to Turner, but is, rather, an effect developed locally by the Kansas City-based singers. The traditional vocal slurs are there, of course, and so too are sustained notes which, combined with a penetrating tone, make casual listening impossible. The audience is involved with the singer, not so much to listen to the words, which often disappear in the driving attack, but by an aural connection few other blues singers have made with their listeners.

His 1938 recording of *Roll 'Em Pete* is the first of many performances of this composition of Pete Johnson's. Through these early years, Turner made excellent recordings with small groups usually featuring, or led by, fine piano players: Johnson, Albert Ammons, Meade Lux Lewis, Willie 'The Lion' Smith, Joe Sullivan, Art Tatum. On all these recordings Joe's driving singing swings musicians who are more than able to swing superbly, even without his encouragement. Not that Joe was incapable of singing reflectively, and movingly, when the material or occasion demanded. Piney Brown, the black manager of the white-owned KC nightspot, the Sunset Club, died in 1940 and Joe and Pete improvised a tribute during a recording session in New York. The result, *Piney Brown Blues*, also became a regular in the Turner-Johnson songbook but Joe never allowed it to lose the qualities which attended its creation.

Univ Wales Swansea

WITHDRAWN FROM STOCK

L.I.S.

SWANSEA

For the most part, however, Joe Turner's singing is imbued with the sheer joy of living.

During the rhythm-and-blues explosion of the 1940s Joe slipped into comparative obscurity but was rescued by a string of minor hits with the black audience, *Chains Of Love, Sweet Sixteen* and then, in 1954, *Shake, Rattle And Roll* which was 'covered' by Bill Haley and thus became a huge success of the white rock 'n' roll boom.

In 1956 Joe Turner recorded an album of his best-known and most-often performed songs. The accompanying band included Pete Johnson, Pete Brown (as), Lawrence Brown (tb) and two members of Basie's All American Rhythm Section, Freddie Green (g) and Walter Page (b). The result was an unqualified success and every one of the superb performances proved to be definitive – *I Want A Little Girl, Wee Baby Blues, Piney Brown Blues*, a superbly rhythmic *Morning Glories* and versions of *Roll 'Em Pete* and *Cherry Red* on which singer and pianist excel themselves.

Later, Joe was picked up by impressario and record company boss Norman Granz and recorded extensively if not always successfully, as his health was by now suspect. Even when backed by men of the calibre of the trumpet kings Roy Eldridge, Dizzy Gillespie and Clark Terry, Joe sometimes failed to measure up. Granz persisted, however, and, amazingly enough, Joe came through the sticky patch which had included hospitalisation in 1981.

On a 1984 set, recorded for Granz in Los Angeles, Joe mostly contented himself with songs from his standard repertoire – *Kansas City Here I Come, Big-Legged Woman* and *Sweet Sixteen*, but also tried his hand at *Time After Time* with excellent results. True, the voice had lost its former power but echoes of majesty abound on a hugely enjoyable record made doubly pleasurable by the fact that a half century on from his Kansas City beginnings, Big Joe Turner was still around to entertain. Sadly, time had almost run out for Big Joe who died in November 1985, the last of the Kansas City blues shouters.

Inevitably, the shadow cast by Little Jimmy Rushing and Big Joe Turner has obscured a number of fine singers, among them Walter

Joe Turner – forcefully majestic.

Brown, Big Miller and, carrying on the tradition to the present day, Eddie Vinson, Joe Williams, Jimmy Witherspoon and others.

Walter Brown (*c*.1917–*c*.1956) inadvertently put the Jay McShann band into the big time. An undistinguished singer, he had a runaway success with his 1941 recording of *Confessin' The Blues* and thereafter became the band's main attraction. In fact, the band was far from being merely a supporting vehicle. It had a fine, swinging rhythm section: McShann (p), Lucky Enois (g), Gene Ramey (b) and Gus Johnson (d), and, of course, in the saxophone section was the as yet unformed genius who was destined to become the next great mover and shaper of jazz – Charlie Parker. It was on a recording of another Walter Brown song, *Hootie's Blues*, that Parker's genius first displayed itself to the ears of a discerning few when he superbly cued the singer's solo. It was a sign of things to come but, for a while at least, Walter Brown, flaws and all, was the McShann band's main man.

Big Miller (1922–) first came to public notice in 1948 when he toured with Lionel Hampton and his Orchestra. The following year found him touring again, this time with the Jay McShann band, and in the early 1950s he was still touring, now with Duke Ellington. Since then he has sung with numerous small groups, including those of Rex Stewart, Nat Pierce and Budd Johnson. A very fine singer, basically in the Kansas City style, his recordings are largely unavailable. Since the 1960s he has worked mostly in Canada which has also aided his comparative, and very undeserved, obscurity to the wider world.

Hot Lips Page (1908–54) was also markedly underrated both as a trumpet player and as a singer by all but his fellow musicians. At its best his vocalising ranks with that of Rushing and Turner. He sings superbly on his 1940 versions of *Evil Man's Blues*, *Just Another Woman*, *My Fightin' Gal* and *Do It If You Wanna*, and is in equally good voice on *Double Trouble Blues* and *I Got What It Takes* recorded in 1944. Excellent examples of Page at his greatest are heard on the V-Disc recordings of *Miss Martingale* and *The Sheik Of Araby* where he is accompanied by an all-star line-up including Bobby Hackett (tp) and Jack Teagarden (tb).

An entertainer well known on the TOBA circuit and a favourite of the Apollo audiences was Pigmeat Markham (1903–81). In the

1920s he toured the South with the tent shows of Ma Rainey and Gonzal White. Generally considered as an eccentric dancer and comedian, Markham's recordings for Blue Note in the 1940s proved him to be a blues shouter of considerable talent. His tough and powerful performances were ably backed by a group led by Oliver Mesheux (tp) which included trombonist Sandy Williams. Markham's nickname originated from a line he delivered during his act: 'I'm sweet Papa Pigmeat, I've got the River Jordan in my hips, and all the women is rarin' to be baptized.' In 1968 he enjoyed renewed fame with an international hit, *Here Comes The Judge*.

Eddie 'Cleanhead' Vinson (1917–) is a fine blues shouter and alto saxophonist out of Texas. For a number of years he played in Milt Larkins' band alongside tenor saxophonists Arnett Cobb and Illinois Jacquet. In 1940 he toured with Bill Broonzy and Lil Green and was then featured with the Cootie Williams Orchestra. In the late-1940s he had some success in the rhythm-and-blues field with such songs as *Kidney Stew Blues* and *Queen Bee Blues*. His eloquent and personal style is heard to good advantage on *Person To Person* and *My Big Brass Bed Is Gone*. His use of the strangulated note at the end of each line makes his singing easily identifiable, as on *Somebody Done Stole My Cherry Red*. He is heard to best advantage shouting above the blues riffs of a driving band. He has influenced a number of singers, including Joe Williams who has smoothed out Vinson's style and adapted it for a more sophisticated market.

Despite his smoothness and sophistication, Joe Williams (1918–) brings to his work a great sense of the meaning of the blues yet is much more accessible to the general public than most of his peers.

In the mid-1950s Joe worked extensively with Basie where singer and band continually struck sparks off one another. When Basie backed Joe on *Every Day*, *Alright, OK, You Win* and *Roll 'Em Pete* the singer was lifted – but never out of the groove. Indeed, listening to singer and band dig into *Comeback* is a salutory experience in jazz musicianship.

In the late 1950s, Joe and the Count continued their working relationship and excellent recordings flowed: *Shake Rattle And Roll* did exactly that while *Cherry Red* glowed. By way of contrast, Joe recorded with a Basie-led small group during the same period, producing fine versions of two Fats Waller songs – *Honeysuckle Rose* and *Ain't Misbehavin'*, and slow but langorously swinging performances of *Dinah* and *If I Could Be With You One Hour Tonight*.

Eventually taking the solo route, Joe Williams found his career flourishing and he became a popular figure in jazz clubs and at festivals and concerts the world over. In the 1970s he was happily testing himself against the somewhat more modern, but heavily blues-influenced playing of the Adderley brothers. A record date in 1973 produced a selection of songs from a wide range of musical origins on all of which Joe was comfortably at home: *Tell Me Where To Scratch* and *Goin' To Chicago* are the blues, *Heritage* is an obscure Duke Ellington song, while *Sad Song* is a superb swinger.

Joe's voice, rich and warm, inevitably mellows the harder edge of the blues and he is, perhaps, better regarded as a blues-influenced jazz singer rather than an out-and-out bluesman.

Jimmy Witherspoon (1923–), although a dozen years younger than Joe Turner, consistently demonstrates similar traditions. He worked with Jay McShann's small groups in the mid-1940s and in countless run-down clubs. It was not a good time, but he was building a repertoire and learning how to tough it out in the face of public disinterest.

At the 1959 Monterey Jazz Festival, Jimmy was accompanied by a truly all-star line-up, including Roy Eldridge (tp), Urbie Green (tb), Woody Herman (cl), Coleman Hawkins and Ben Webster (ts) and Earl Hines (p). The singer made an enormous impact on the huge crowd, with fine performances of *'T'Ain't Nobody's Biz-ness If I Do*, which is a 'Spoon standard, *When I've Been Drinkin'* and *There's Good Rockin' Tonight* – and there was. After the concert, Jimmy Witherspoon's career blossomed and all the years of playing two-bit dives finally paid off.

A concert, recorded at the Olympia in Paris in April 1961, included superb versions of *'T'Ain't Nobody's Biz-ness*, *Times Gettin' Tougher Than Tough* (a permanent feature in the 'Spoon repertoire even if times, for the singer, ain't as tough as they were) and *Gee, Baby, Ain't I Good To You*, with masterly playing from Buck Clayton (tp), Buddy Tate (ts) and Sir Charles Thompson (p). A climactic *Roll 'Em Pete* had the French audience, never known for their restraint at any jazz concert, screaming for more.

A British tour brought him to the Bull's Head at Barnes Bridge,

Joe Williams – smoothly swinging.

London in 1966 where a sparkling set, fortunately recorded, teamed him with a band which included Dick Morrissey (ts) and Phil Seaman (d).

Witherspoon's career continued through the rest of the 1960s and 1970s and into the next decade. An excellent recording session, again in Paris but in 1980, teamed him with Panama Francis and the Savoy Sultans. Although the material was familiar, the verve and enthusiasm of the singer and the superbly swinging Sultans made this a memorable occasion.

Then, illness threatened to end his career, if not his life. Fortunately, a throat operation in Manchester, England restored him to good health and left him not merely in good voice but, if anything, with a wider vocal range than before. As the singer himself has observed, he can now hit some low notes that were previously outside his compass.

Ernie Andrews (1927–) is a blues-influenced singer who regularly sings today with the Capp-Pierce Juggernaut in Los Angeles. When digging into material like *Roll 'Em Pete*, *Wee Baby Blues* or *Every Day I Have The Blues* there is a mutual response similar to that enjoyed in the past by Joe Williams and the Basie band. Ernie Andrews' blues inflections give added texture to some of the more popular items from the Duke Ellington songbook – *Satin Doll*, *Sophisticated Lady* and *Don't Get Around Much Anymore*. One of his own favourite albums was recorded with Cannonball Adderley. He does, however, display an occasional weakness for popular material which is best left out of the jazz blues singer's repertoire.

Of this group of singers, the KC-shouters their contemporaries and descendants, only Jimmy Rushing and Helen Humes worked for any length of time within one of the big bands in the black half of the Swing Era. This was a period when every band had a singer, or two if they could afford them. Although they came for the most part from a different tradition, there were several other black singers worthy of considered attention.

June Richmond (1915–62) sang with the Jimmy Dorsey band in 1938, becoming one of the first black singers to work regularly with a white band (Billie Holiday was briefly with Artie Shaw also in 1938). June had little subtlety but in the right context her strident KC-based shouting voice could prove satisfactory. She was heard to

Jimmy Witherspoon – tough enthusiasm.

best advantage in the 1940s when she worked with the Andy Kirk band.

Rosetta Tharpe sang with the Lucky Millinder band and enjoyed a separate and longer-lasting career as a gospel singer of distinction (and will be dealt with in Chapter 5 of this book). Ella was with Chick Webb, of course, and during the tag-end of the 1930s and on through the early 1940s several notable singers worked with big bands: Pearl Bailey was with Cootie Williams before becoming internationally known as a talented comedienne and actress; Dinah Washington and Sarah Vaughan were paying their dues too before becoming major stylists and achieving great success (they, with Ella, are dealt with in Chapter 4).

The names of only a few black male big band singers linger on: Pha Terrell (1910–45) was with Andy Kirk and his Clouds of Joy (not exactly a big band even though they often managed to sound as if they were). Dan Grissom was with Jimmie Lunceford, although trombonist Trummy Young was more attuned to jazz as his occasional singing showed. Trummy had a big hit with his own composition, *'T'ain't What You Do It's The Way That You Do It*. Sonny Parker, a powerful blues balladeer, first found fame with his 1949 recording, *Drinking Wine Spoo Dee Oo Dee*, made with Lionel Hampton. Herb Jeffries and Al Hibbler made only a small mark during their stints with Duke Ellington.

Given the enormous number of marvellous songs he wrote, Duke Ellington's taste in singers seems to have been remarkably unsatisfactory. Really, only Ivie Anderson (1904–49) was above average and, probably through automatic grouping with the other Ellington singers, is usually overlooked or, at best, underrated. Ivie had a simple and straightforward vocal style and always displayed concern for the melodic qualities of her material. Her recording with Ellington in 1932 of *It Don't Mean A Thing If It Ain't Got That Swing* set a standard for singers no other Ellingtonian ever attained. On *Old Plantation* and *All God's Chillun Got Rhythm*, recorded under her own name, she sings with a delightfully rhythmic ease which rises above the mildly dubious nature of the material. Whether singing popular songs of the day, or Duke's own compositions, Ivie imbued her work with her own impeccable taste. Her successors with Duke included Joya Sherrill, Kay Davis and Maria Ellington but Ivie was, by far, the best.

Impeccable taste was embodied in the work of another fine singer who started out in the 1930s. Unlike Ivie Anderson, who died young, she sang on into the 1980s although there were one or two 'retirements' along the way. Maxine Sullivan (1911–) came from a highly musical family, as she would later demonstrate by her remarkable gifts for learning to play a variety of musical instruments. While working with the Ina Ray Hutton band Maxine was introduced to pianist-bandleader Claude Thornhill. This was in 1938 and together they made a few sides, some of which received scant attention from the record company, let alone the public, although one, *Stop, You're Breaking My Heart*, really deserved much better treatment. Of the others there was a good *Gone With The Wind* and an arrangement of a Scottish song which any gambler on hits would have marked down as a rank outsider. For reasons best known to the record-buying public, *Loch Lomond* was a smash. Ever afterwards, Maxine's repertoire was littered with songs of vaguely Scottish folk origin, among them *Annie Laurie*. Helped along by the unlikely success of *Loch Lomond*, Maxine became enormously popular in the 1930s and worked through into the 1940s both as a single and with various bands including those of John Kirby, to whom she was married for a while, and Benny Carter with whom she made a fine version of *What A Difference A Day Makes* in 1941.

A singer of extreme delicacy and charm, it is clear from Maxine's work that she was influenced by Ethel Waters with whom she shares marked stylistic devices. In the late 1940s she appeared in London but by the 1950s her quiet style of singing was out of fashion and after a serious illness she retired. Heavily involved in community work, Maxine channeled much of her energies into 'the House that Jazz Built', a property in the Bronx. The house, which is a museum, is dedicated to the memory of her second husband, stride pianist Cliff Jackson.

At the end of the 1960s she came out of retirement and proved she had lost none of her talent when she recorded two albums with saxophonist-arranger Bob Wilber. One of the albums is devoted to the songs of Hoagy Carmichael and includes fine versions of *Skylark* and *I Get Along Without You Very Well*. On the second album, 'Close as Pages in a Book', she is in delightful form on all tracks with exceptional performances of *Harlem Butterfly*, *Every Time* and *As Long As I Live*.

Wishing to broaden her range, Maxine began playing valve trombone and flugelhorn, eventually settling for the 'pocket' trumpet which is, perhaps, more in keeping with her diminutive stature. She also acted (she had made a number of films early in her career, including an appearance in the 1938 *St Louis Blues*), and was nominated for a Tony Award for her role in a Broadway musical.

With record dates in Sweden in 1981 and concert and festival appearances through into the mid-1980s, Maxine Sullivan shows no signs of tiring or of losing her ability to perform songs with great feeling and, in her own words, is 'back in business to stay'.

Unlike Maxine Sullivan, many fine singers of the 1930s and 1940s are almost completely forgotten today. These now unfashionable artists lack due appreciation perhaps because their wry asides and gentle swing appear mild and innocuous to the casual listener. Limited in range, yet extremely stylish and expressive, these singers are unpretentious but highly individualistic. They drew their inspiration from diverse sources: classic blues, vaudeville, jazz, and popular song. They sing naturally and without affectation, yet with awareness and style. All are evocative storytellers, singing not of lost love but of lost lovers, of good times as well as bad, of bad luck and strong liquor.

Georgia White (1903-unk.) offers a humorous slice of urban teenage life in *Was I Drunk?*, a cautionary tale which tells of a young girl plaintively 'wishing to see what in life I'd missed'. She soon 'met a youth, a bit uncouth', and ends, somewhat dispassionately, with, 'he said give so I gave; after all, what was I saving?' Georgia White recorded prolifically during the late 1930s. Among her output were *Walkin' The Street, I'll Keep Sittin' On It, The Blues Ain't Nothin' But*, and a hauntingly unusual *Moonshine Blues* all with superb guitar and piano accompaniment. Unobtainable for many years, Georgia White's recordings are now receiving the welcome attention of record producer Rosetta Reitz.

Julia Lee (1902–58) sang with her brother George E. Lee's Novelty Singing Orchestra. Her recording of *Won't You Come Over To My House* contained a sentiment echoed two decades later by Nellie Lutcher's *Hurry On Down*. Julia never received much acclaim, despite being a fine, creative artist. An accomplished pianist, she was very popular on the West Coast nightclub circuit

112

Maxine Sullivan – delicate charm.

(*Centre*) Cleo Brown; (*clockwise from top left*) Julia Lee, Lil Green, Rosetta Howard, Memphis Minnie, Nellie Lutcher, Georgia White.

but was best-known in and around Kansas City where she held several long residencies. Her *Decent Woman Blues* and *He's Tall Dark And Handsome* are fine examples of a talented singer whose work is now also being reissued.

At age fourteen, Nellie Lutcher (1915–) played piano with the Clarence Hart band (which also was home for a while to Bunk Johnson, the legendary New Orleans trumpet-player rescued from obscurity in the 1940s revival). Nellie became an 'overnight' success in 1947 and a string of hit records followed: *Fine Brown Frame, My Mother's Eyes, He's A Real Gone Guy* and, of course, *Hurry On Down*. Not steeped in the blues, Nellie's singing has a joyous ring which, when added to her jazz-style piano-playing makes her a highly entertaining peformer. Her records too have been subject to reissue.

The unique, personable style of Lil Green (1919–54) captivated black American audiences during the war years. Her recordings of *Give Your Mama One Smile, What's the Matter With Love, Oh, Babe* and *Romance In The Dark*, which was her most successful song, all have the benefit of excellent support from pianist Simeon Henry and Big Bill Broonzy on guitar. These were forerunners for recordings by such artists as Dinah Washington, Ruth Brown and others. Indeed, Lil's definitive performance of the sardonic *Why Don't You Do Right?* paved the way for Peggy Lee's enormously successful cover version.

There were numerous other fine female vocalists of this period: Merline Johnson, the Yas-Yas Girl, who recorded somewhat unevenly with Chicago-based bluesmen; Rosetta Crawford, a contemporary of Bessie Smith's, who was not 'discovered' until 1940 despite having a wonderful sense of timing and a wryly humorous manner reminiscent of Sophie Tucker; Rosetta Howard worked with the Morand-Rand band in Chicago before gaining success in New York. Her singing was very much in the vaudeville tradition but was, nevertheless, built upon a solid rhythmic sense.

There was also Kansas Katie who made only a handful of records which show a marked similarity to Lil Green's style. Nora Lee King was even less well-served by record companies but in the 1980s appeared with the Harlem Blues and Jazz Band. The evocatively named Bea Booze was another fine blues shouter whose firm voice was heard to good effect on her Brunswick recordings where she was accompanied by some exceptionally sound blues piano. Unlike some of the other singers whose work is being reissued in the 1980s, Bea's recordings still languish in record company vaults.

Hazel Scott was a sparkling pianist whose singing style was clearly influenced by Billie Holiday. Another gifted piano-player, this time in the boogie-woogie tradition, was Cleo Brown whose success in Chicago in the 1930s led to her having her own radio show. She had a small, plaintive voice and was followed by Rose Murphy who took this particular quality of her singing towards the borders of parody. Rose developed a childlike falsetto which gained her a substantial following with hits, including *Busy Line*, in the late 1940s. And there was also the limited, but nevertheless attractive voice of Blue Lu Barker who advised the ladies to *Never Brag About Your Man*, urged on by the incisive trumpet of Red Allen. Then there was Mae Barnes who sang with strong jazz feeling and extremely good timing as can be heard on her version of *True Blue Lou*. Albinia Jones sang the blues with a whining, nasal delivery and can be heard on a good, updated version of *Evil Gal Blues*. Gladys Bentley's career began in the 1920s and continued through the next two decades. Accompanying herself at the piano, she included male impersonation in her act which she performed at The Cotton Club and Connie's Inn in the 1930s. Langston Hughes described her as 'a perfect piece of African sculpture' and went on to comment on the fiercely rhythmic manner in which she beat time by pounding her large feet on the floor.

A small number of white singers also adopted the jazz-influenced cabaret style. They included Frances Faye who was a female equivalent of Louis Prima and, although she sang with little depth, her great spirit earned her the mildly questionable nickname of Frantic Fanny. Another was Ella Mae Morse who enjoyed brief fame thanks to her recording of *Cow Cow Boogie* with Freddie Slack. A few years on, Her Nibs Miss Georgia Gibbs followed this same tradition.

In a more orthodox mould was Viola Wells (1902–84), better known to her many admirers as Miss Rhapsody, who entered vaudeville, graduated to travelling shows, and sang with Ida Cox for a while with Ida's own band. At ease with the blues and with sacred music, Miss Rhapsody was a gritty survivior. She suffered from advanced diabetes and at one point in her career lost a leg in an accident. She recorded in the 1940s and was still recording three decades on. Interestingly, her many recordings include two of her own compositions: *Bye Bye Baby* and *My Lucky Day* and she also recorded a fine lyrical version of *After You've Gone*, for once, thankfully, sung as a ballad, and *Sweet Man*. Unlike those other ladies, many of whom were treated with scant regard for their undoubted talents during their lifetimes, Miss Rhapsody did receive some of the attention due to her even if, mostly, it came late in her career. Clyde Bernhardt, with whom Miss Rhapsody recorded and toured, was also a good blues shouter in addition to being a fine trombonist.

If the attention of the public at large was diverted from these many fine singers of the late 1930s and early 1940s some allowance can be made. After all, this was the Swing Era and the spotlight was firmly on the big bands, and, for the most part, the white big bands at that.

Of the many commercial aspects of popular singing from this period, the one most readily associated with jazz in the general public's mind was the big band singer. On stage with the countless bands aspiring to match the success of Benny Goodman would always be a pretty canary in a party dress who warbled currently popular songs. Although the black bands, and hence black singers, had a share in this bonanza, the real commercial gains were made by white bands, and their singers were the ones who drew most public attention. It must be stressed that the jazz content of the majority of the many hundreds of name bands of this period was decidedly variable. For the most part their singers stood well outside the jazz tradition although jazz phrasing had now become commonplace, if only rarely accomplished with any degree of success.

Among the white female singers of the big band days were some who enjoyed transient success, others faded before they had time to blossom fully either because they were simply not good enough, or found the tough life of one-night stands too much, or decided to marry (often members of the band).

Helen O'Connell was a bright asset for Jimmy Dorsey and had a massive hit with *Green Eyes* on which she shared vocal honours with Bob Eberly. She also worked with Artie Shaw during Billie Holiday's brief stint with the band. Through no fault of her own, Helen's vocals were featured at the expense of Billie's during radio broadcasts when sponsors decreed that their products should not be associated with a black singer. Mary Ann McCall, who sang with Tommy Dorsey and Charlie Barnet, began as a decidedly run-of-the-mill band singer but matured remarkably in the late 1940s during her second stint with Woody Herman's band. She drew appreciation from jazzmen, thanks to her stylistic originality and wit and her ability to sing with a rare quality of unsentimental worldliness. She recorded with bebop musicians Howard McGhee, Dexter Gordon and Al Cohn. Helen Forrest was an able singer, certainly above average but, unlike Mary Ann McCall, proved unable to make the leap into the modernist camp after spells with the bands of Harry James, Benny Goodman and Artie Shaw. She returned to the record studios in 1983 but, despite the spirited accompaniment of a swinging little band, the results were disappointing.

Helen Ward also returned to the recording studios long after her Swing Era career, during which she sang with Benny Goodman, was over. This was in 1979 and the results, although tastefully pleasant, failed to recapture the singer's earlier qualities. Kay Starr's break came as substitute for Marion Hutton with the Glenn Miller Orchestra. She later sang with the bands of Bob Crosby and Joe Venuti. In 1944 she had her first big hit with Charlie Barnet, *Share Croppin' Blues*. A strong, pleasant-voiced singer, somewhat reminiscent of Dinah Washington in tone and delivery, Kay's early training with jazz groups left an indelible impression on her singing style which survived through her popular successes of the 1950s.

As the 1930s gave way to the 1940s and the Swing Era continued its brief life, other singers emerged, many of whom developed into mature song stylists (and who will be dealt with in Chapter 4).

A number of excellent singers worked with the Stan Kenton Orchestra, a sometimes huge and occasionally unwieldy organisation which many thought signalled the end of the big bands, if not of jazz itself. Kenton had a good ear for girl singers (one of the first he hired was Anita O'Day) and perhaps the young woman most readily associated with the music of Stan the Man is June Christy.

Possessor of a dry, husky voice, June Christy (1925–) is at her best when backed by a powerhouse big band. A relaxed and seasoned performer, albeit with occasionally slightly suspect pitching, June's bright and bubbly personality glows through her singing. Particularly effective on up-tempo numbers and on the Latin-tinge songs, like *Tampico*, which Kenton and his arrangers always favoured, she could also handle a ballad most satisfactorily. On *Willow Weep For Me, Soothe Me* and *He's Funny That Way*, June showed a marked appreciation for the nuances of the lyric and her innate sense of fun shone through *His Feet's Too Big For De Bed* and *I Told Ya I Loved Ya*.

June married a member of the Kenton band, tenor saxophonist Bob Cooper, and made some excellent recordings with his small groups in the mid-1940s. A good version of *How High The Moon* resulted, as did fine interpretations of *What's New?* and *Prelude To A Kiss*, and bouncy performances of *Wrap Your Troubles In Dreams, I*

June Christy – bright and bubbly.

Can't Give You Anything But Love and *Lullaby In Rhythm*.

After some years in retirement, June was booked to appear in Holland at the 1985 North Sea Jazz Festival.

Following June in the Kenton band came Jerri Winters and Chris Connor, both very good singers, but at the time of their stints with Kenton relatively inexperienced. A few years on and Chris Connor had developed into a stylish singer with an intense feel for jazz. Her choice of material was not always faultless but, unlike many of her contemporaries, she had learned to disregard valueless lyrics in favour of creating a jazz interpretation of the music. She was well served on a 1978 recording date which includes sensitive versions of *When Sonny Gets Blue* and *Here's That Rainy Day* alongside swinging accounts of *I Feel A Song Coming On* and *Things Are Swinging*.

Ruth Price sings in a style reminiscent of both June Christy and Chris Connor but her voice is thinner and occasionally poorly pitched. Nevertheless, she manages to overcome these deficiencies through performances of considerable vitality.

Among the male singers with the white swing (and sweet) bands of the 1930s and 1940s were Frank Sinatra (first with Harry James, later with Tommy Dorsey), Dick Haymes (Sinatra's successor with James), Bob Eberly (with Jimmy Dorsey) and his brother Ray Eberle (with Glenn Miller) and Perry Como (with Ted Weems).

Quite clearly these singers are well removed from the jazz lineage yet some, Sinatra especially, owe jazz an undeniable debt. After leaving Harry James, Sinatra (1915–) joined Tommy Dorsey, from whose trombone playing he consciously learned breathing, dynamics and jazz phrasing. Despite his astonishing success among pubescent bobby-soxers with songs like *I'll Be Seeing You* and *Fools Rush In*, it is Sinatra's work on many other songs which reveal him at his early best. *Without A Song* (an unlikely vehicle), *Blue Skies, In The Blue Of The Evening* and several songs which became permanent features of the Sinatra repertoire: *Be Careful It's My Heart, Violets For Your Furs, The Sunshine Of Your Smile* and *How About You?*.

Apart from his close study of Dorsey's trombone playing, Sinatra has acknowledged his debt to Billie Holiday and Mabel Mercer. Although he cannot be regarded as a jazz singer, his singing style is directly derived from jazz and he has always been at his best when backed by jazz musicians. Above all, he extended popular singing from the 2/4 style of Crosby to the 4/4 beat of swing.

Generally speaking, the big band singers moved steadily away from the jazz world and, as that world was undergoing a revolution, there were soon few opportunities for singers with genuine jazz roots. The recording ban called by the American Federation of Musicians, which took effect in July 1942 and continued on through to 1944, proved a blessing in disguise for singers. They could still record but as solo artists, often backed by choirs. Many of them prospered: Sinatra, of course, and Como and Haymes, also Doris Day and innumerable others whose qualities were variable and whose jazz connections were, at best, tenuous.

It was bebop, however, which was steering jazz into new, and for some decidedly choppy, waters. The musicians participating in the revolution gathered in small subversive groups in such underground centres as Minton's Playhouse in New York where they plotted the overthrow of the kings of swing. Their new, experimental music was hard to play, to identify with, and even to label. It was be-bop, re-bop, bebop, and eventually just bop.

The fans either loved it or they hated it and, not surprisingly, the record companies were wary. The new music was never really singers' music but there were some who tried, and a few became adept if not wholly successful.

Leo Watson (1898–1950), although not himself a bebop musician, was the inspiration for many of the hip singers who emerged in the 1940s. A scat singer with a highly personal manner, he would improvise his scat lines as if he were, say, a trombonist. Initially he became well known along 52nd Street during the 1930s when he appeared at many clubs with the Spirits of Rhythm. The group's successes included *We've Got The Blues*, *My Old Man* and *I'll Be Ready When The Great Day Comes*. Watson recorded with a number of big bands in the Swing Era, including those of Artie Shaw and Gene Krupa, but was at his considerable best in the small group setting which allowed freer rein to his ingenious improvising.

Epitome of the hip 1940s zoot-suited performer was Harry 'The Hipster' Gibson a club singer-pianist whose way-out repertoire included such gems as *Who Put The Benzedrine In Mrs Murphy's Ovaltine?*, *Zoot Gibson Rides Again* and *I Stay Brown All Year Round*. Gibson's formidable repertoire of comic songs and patter

Slim Gaillard –
surrealist supreme.

made a marked impression upon such notable stand-up comedians as Lord Buckley and Lenny Bruce.

Slim Gaillard (1916–) is a man of astonishing verbal dexterity who came to the attention of bemused fans in the New York clubs where he often worked with bass-player Slam Stewart (who developed a novel style of humming an improvised solo in unison with his own bowed bass playing). Slim Gaillard was a surrealist who, had he been in almost any other branch of the arts, would have been hailed as a great innovator. He created a new language which only the hip could understand (and even they were not always too sure). This language, known as Vout, allowed him to compose, often instantaneously, weird, yet curiously logical fantasy tales which were superbly rhythmic. He had major hits with *Flat Foot Floogie* and *Cement Mixer* and remains unique among jazzmen as being composer and lyricist of a classic children's nursery rhyme: *Down By The Station*. Now resident in London, Slim continues to delight and amaze and has acquired a new generation of fans, or Voutereenies.

Although Gaillard was supreme, the term surrealist can also applied to Babs Gonzales (1919–80). More a bebopper than a hipster, Gonzales's scat singing is heard to advantage on such classic performances as *Professor Bop*, *Cool Whaling* and the hilarious *Me Spelled M E, Me*. His voice was harsh and gravelly and he had a poor sense of pitch but his timing was excellent and he had a good sense of harmony. His hip monologues were an entertaining part of his performance.

Just as Dizzy Gillespie's trumpet roots go back to Louis Armstrong by way of Roy Eldridge, so Joe Carroll's roots return to the same source by way of Leo Watson. Carroll had a hard, rough-toned voice with a limited range and lacks Watson's subtlety but performs with an exuberant swing. Perhaps the earliest of the bebop singers, he is heard at his best on songs like *School Days* and *Oo Shoo Bee Doo Bee*.

Eddie Jefferson was the least self-conscious of the exponents of vocalese, the natural extension of bebop singing. He is also generally regarded as the first singer to fashion words to solos originally played by top jazz musicians, thus creating vocalese. Jefferson's lyrics to James Moody's solo on *I'm In The Mood For Love* gained King Pleasure great success. Both Jefferson and King Pleasure sang with engaging wit and could accurately shape words to instrumental solos. Both were highly inventive performers with keen harmonic sense.

Unlike most other areas of jazz singing, in bebop the men seemed to have the edge, although Betty Roché proved a fine exponent of scatting. A female counterpart to Joe Carroll, she is best remembered for her extended scat introduction to an early-1950s version of *Take The A Train* with the Duke Ellington Orchestra, together with a number of excellent but generally unavailable solo albums.

As with most new departures in jazz, just who began bop singing is open to question. As suggested, Joe Carroll was one of the earliest but credit is often given to Dave Lambert and Buddy Stewart who sang with the Gene Krupa band in the mid-1940s. Lambert (1917–66) later formed the Lambert Singers and his New York apartment became a centre for singers where vocal jam sessions were commonplace, with singers trading choruses and phrases as would jazz instrumentalists. Along with Jon Hendricks and Scottish-born

Annie Ross, Lambert then attracted great attention with vocalised arrangements of Count Basie classics. Lambert, Hendricks and Ross were superbly equipped and well-rehearsed and their conception, with judicious use of multi-tracking, was excellent. The two men would sing the reed and trombone parts with Annie Ross taking the trumpets and the occasional piano solo.

Of the three it was Annie (1930–) who was the natural swinger. As a solo performer in her own right, she is a relaxed singer with an oblique and occasionally rather blasé style. Her decision to leave singing for an acting career (and a somewhat subdued one at that, following personal tragedy) has taken a rare talent from the jazz scene. Annie had earlier acting experience as a child in Hollywood where she lived with her aunt, Ella Logan, who recorded with the Spirits of Rhythm.

Another group from the bebop period was the duo of Jackie Cain and Roy Kral who worked with Charlie Ventura's 'Bop for the People' band towards the end of the 1940s. As the umbrella group's name suggests this was bebop modified to be more accessible to the wider public. The singers' version of bop singing was similarly modified but was, nevertheless, imaginative and highly polished. Their impeccable flights of fancy are heard on such songs as *Spring Can Really Hang You Up The Most* and *I Wish I Were In Love Again*. Cain and Kral were still recording in the 1980s. Roy's sister, Irene Kral, sang in a similar manner to Jackie Cain and proved to be a stylish singer with a taste for superior material.

The singing groups of the 1940s were by no means restricted to the beboppers. There were many whose close-harmony style more closely resembled much earlier traditions of American song. The Mills Brothers were an excellent jazz-influenced group. The four men (originally four brothers but when one died their father stepped in) added lustre to innumerable popular songs of the war years and recorded with many other artists, including Louis Armstrong and Ella Fitzgerald. In the late 1970s they reformed, now only the brothers were left, and wowed audiences in Europe with their effortlessly stylish singing.

For a time even better known than the Mills Brothers, though much less jazz-orientated, were the Ink Spots. They began as a hot group but eventually became over-stylised through use of falsetto singing and spoken bass monologues. In later years the Four Freshmen worked in an effective modern manner; the Hi-Los were clever and efficient vocalists who took the Freshmen's style on to evermore brilliant vocal gymnastics; Singers Unlimited continued the vocal group tradition on the edges of jazz, while in the more popular field the work of Manhattan Transfer and Rare Silk echoes similar origins.

The hip singer as cabaret act has produced a number of worthy performers. Oscar Brown was never quite a jazz singer but gives inspired interpretations of his own hip lyrics. Mose Allison has a style reminiscent of Hoagy Carmichael with overtones of the blues. Blossom Dearie is highly regarded by songwriters who hear in her performances exactly what they hoped to hear when they wrote their songs. Bob Dorough is another highly regarded singer whose work is greatly enjoyed by American audiences.

Of this group, the most tightly linked to the jazz scene is Dave Frishberg (1933–) who also favours Carmichael's music. An excellent pianist, songwriter and cunning lyricist, Dave imbues his own material with warmth and hip charm, giving it a unique personal identity. Whether singing of lost lovers or such unlikely subjects as his accountant or White Castle beer, he has a remarkable gift for inner rhymes while his piano playing, with its echoes of the stride giants of the past, is always masterly.

What the best of these singers, the hipsters, the groups, the big band singers, had in common was style. The most stylish of them all, however, transcended the limited boundaries imposed externally upon jazz. These were singers with whom even the wholly non-jazz public could comfortably identify. As a result, most of them achieved fame, and some fortune. These are the song-stylists.

4 *Smooth, Swinging and Stylish*

The rise of the jazz-influenced solo singer began taking identifiable shape in the second half of the 1940s although, with hindsight, its origins are clear to see earlier in the Swing Era. Singers with the big bands became as much an attraction as the instrumentalists had been at the start of the Era: Sinatra with Tommy Dorsey, Peggy Lee with Benny Goodman, Anita O'Day with Gene Krupa, Dinah Washington with Lionel Hampton, Ella Fitzgerald with Chick Webb, and many, many more.

After World War 2 several factors affected the music business, all contributing in some measure towards change. Patterns of entertainment altered; among other things people in America stayed home to watch TV instead of going to the movies or visiting dance halls. Even simpler, but impossible to define or explain, people's tastes changed. They wanted something new.

In jazz, of course, there was the bebop revolution but this was too esoteric for most of the ordinary fans. That was not what they wanted but, so it seemed, neither did they want the big bands. The big bands began to fold just before the middle of the decade; by its end, they were as rare as dinosaurs, and just as difficult to sustain. Contributing to the decline in their popularity was the fact that for a time the fans could not buy new records by the bands, simply because such records were no longer being made. The American Federation of Musicians had called for a recording ban in order to gain for musicians a share of the enormous profits being made by record companies on sales of the countless band records made during the Swing Era. Usually (but not always), the band leader had a royalty agreement while the sidemen in the band received union scale for the session. If leaders and managers could get away with it, the musicians were paid less than scale. As this was the Depression and jobs were not to be jeopardised for sake of a few dollars, pay often was worse than it should have been. The AF of M wanted a better deal and under the guidance (or, as it turned out, misguidance) of the union president, James Caesar Petrillo, negotiations degenerated into a ban. By the time the ban crumbled the big band era was on the slide and the musicians lost out anyway. Singers, however, were another matter.

As seen, the recording ban did not apply to them and they took full advantage of a situation which placed them in great demand. For the record companies, singers were manna from heaven. Singers could work with the house pianist or a chorus or accompany themselves on piano. They cost less, they were easy to promote, they had established, extensive repertoires, they could learn and rehearse new songs with less trouble than a fifteen piece band. Most important, regardless of age, they were highly skilled and musically mature. Their years of on-the-road training were finally paying off.

For the fans, the singers appeared to fill their needs. They were already familiar with them from their earlier recordings, broadcasts and live appearances with the bands. In any event, by the time the record companies had finished their promotion campaigns, the fans were sure that this was what they wanted. Maybe it was. Certainly, singers were in.

Fortunately, many were strongly jazz-influenced and were already incipient stylists of American popular song. A select few were real jazz singers. Doyenne of these singers was, and for many still is, Ella Fitzgerald.

Ella Fitzgerald (1918–) was born in Newport News, Virginia, moved to New York while still a child, and was orphaned at the age of fifteen. Ella wanted to be a dancer and entered a talent contest with that in mind. She was not very good and suffered the indignity of being booed off. Then she tried again, at the Harlem Opera House and at the Apollo Theatre where the audience was never afraid to let its opinions be known. This time, however, there was no danger of rejection because she went on not as a dancer but as a singer. Ella was an enormous success and, more importantly, she was heard by some of the right people. Just who recommended the slightly overweight young girl to bandleader Chick Webb is open to doubt. As the years passed and her fame grew, several people took credit for the introduction. The details do not matter. What is important is that Webb listened, a trifle unwillingly for Ella did not look like anyone's idea of a big band singer, liked what he heard and hired her. This was in 1935 when she was still only 17.

Ella's first recording with the Chick Webb band, made that first year, was *Love And Kisses*. Webb featured her on popular numbers of the day: *Sing Me A Swing Song, Rock It For Me, My Heart Belongs To Daddy, Undecided*. The combination of Ella's sweet lyricism and Chick's driving rhythm made a phenomenal partnership. The recordings flowed and her first major hit was the nonsense song *A-Tisket, A-Tasket*, an adaptation of an old nursery rhyme which she recorded in 1938. Ella herself adapted the lyric to a tune by Al Freeman, the whole thing being cooked up to cheer the chronically sick Webb who was undergoing one of his frequent spells of hospitalisation.

When Webb died in June 1939, Ella fronted the band (the baton had been in the hands of Bardu Ali for some years, thus leaving the crippled Webb to remain seated behind his drums) and kept things going for another two years, all the while recording prolifically. Among the successes were *Baby Won't You Please Come Home* and *Cabin In The Sky*, but she occasionally sank to such peurile rubbish as *My Wubba Dolly* and *Melinda The Mousie*.

Eventually disbanding in 1941, Ella continued to record but now as an artist in her own right, although she was frequently featured with commercially successful groups – the Ink Spots, the Mills Brothers, the Delta Rhythm Boys. Many of her recordings were of novelty songs and the poor quality of much of the material pressed on her by Decca stultified her career, but salvation came in the form of the microgroove record.

Long-playing records brought Ella and other quality singers renewed viability as recording artists for there was no longer any need for the instant appeal of the three-minute song. A talented

Ella Fitzgerald – melodic perfection.

singer could now use the length of an album to explore a wide range of moods. For a now-mature stylist like Ella Fitzgerald it was a heaven-sent opportunity.

In 1950 there appeared an album of songs by George Gershwin on which Ella was accompanied by the equally stylish pianist Ellis Larkins. This was the first of many 'songbook' albums she would make and in many respects it remains the best. Unfortunately, the artistic success of the Gershwin album was not followed up by Decca and Ella reverted to recording singles, some of which were good, some mediocre and one, her version of George Shearing's *Lullaby Of Birdland*, was a huge, and possibly unexpected, success.

Since 1946 Ella had been working with Norman Granz's 'Jazz at the Philharmonic' concert package where her ability as a scat singer had been developed. Backed by the cream of the current crop of jazz musicians, such numbers as *Flying Home, How High The Moon* and *Air Mail Special* were guaranteed show-stoppers. Granz had also become her manager but it was not until the early 1950s that he finally succeeded in freeing her from Decca and signing her to his own record label. When he did, jazz fans rejoiced, but Granz had ideas with which many were at first unhappy. Aware of the potential touched upon by the Gershwin album, Granz embarked on the 'songbook series'. This was a long series of albums devoted to the work of Rodgers and Hart, Harold Arlen, Cole Porter, Jerome Kern and the other masters of American popular song. These, and other albums recorded during this period, were with the sometimes bland backing of studio orchestras under the direction of Buddy Bregman, Nelson Riddle, Frank De Vol and others. The jazz critics and many fans were dismayed. In commercial terms, however, the albums were a huge popular success and Ella became an international star. Granz was proved commercially right, thus illustrating why he was so successful where others failed. Beyond doubt these albums caught Ella at the peak of her vocal abilities and the attention paid to her by a new, wider public was entirely merited.

A tough itinerary of world tours was totally successful, public acclaim and commercial success were hers but, for the jazz *afficionado*, her concert performances were often more interesting than her recorded work.

Fortunately, there were also some fine studio recordings strong in jazz content, among them two excellent albums with Louis Armstrong and Oscar Peterson, one with Duke Ellington, and a swinging set with Count Basie. Additionally, there were the recordings of the JATP concerts and, in 1963, a set entitled 'These Are The Blues'. This album included *How Long, How Long Blues*, *See See Rider*, *Cherry Red* and *St Louis Blues*. Accompanied by Roy Eldridge (tp), Ella served these songs well but, as critic David Burnett-James remarked in his review of the album's 1977 reissue, this was 'the blues with the blood wiped off'. Ella's tremendous success was interrupted by illness but in the early 1970s she resumed her recording career. Her voice was no longer as strong or as fluid as in the previous two decades but now more jazz qualities were apparent in her performances. The ease of phrasing remained even if the range was slightly limited, and she used her voice to much more telling effect. The touch of blandness sometimes evident in the songbook era was gone and now, for the first time, she displayed involvement with the lyric.

Ella was now embarked upon her most musically satisfying period. Her performances with such musicians as guitarist Joe Pass, either live or on record, were filled with superb examples of jazz singing at its very best. With her regular accompanist, pianist Tommy Flanagan, she slips easily through the most taxing of material. It may well be that this fluidity is the quality which has counted most against her in assessments made by many jazz critics and fans. That ease of posture and manner is an opaque facade which can lead the unwary into the false assumption that her performances lack depth. Nothing could be further from the truth. Lying behind that calm exterior is thirty years of hard work, training and total dedication to her art. True, there have been times when the jazz content in Ella's work has been slight yet, whatever the context, she has always transmitted a flowing swing which lifts the most turgid material. With quality songs she has invariably produced performances of melodic perfection, although admittedly lacking the intensity of emotion Billie Holiday brought to her songs.

Ella represents the general public's idea of the perfect jazz singer. Even if true jazz enthusiasts continue to argue the point they are still likely to have more than a handful of her records in their collections. And, while they might not agree wholeheartedly with Bing Crosby's oft-quoted maxim, they will probably not argue too stridently against it: 'Man, woman or child, Ella's the greatest'.

Ella Fitzgerald was far from being the only singer to enter show business by way of New York's Harlem talent contests. In 1943 a nineteen-year-old hopeful ventured there, undoubtedly aware of what the already-successful Ella had achieved in the past eight years. This newcomer's success followed a strikingly similar pattern. She too was heard at a contest. Singer Billy Eckstine, then with the Earl Hines band who were appearing at the Apollo, recommended her to his boss and within a few days she was alongside him on the bandstand.

Sarah Vaughan (1924–) was born in Newark, New Jersey, into a musical family. A highly skilled pianist, she approached music thoughtfully and analytically, and from a very early age was demonstrating a considerable degree of original thought as a singer.

When Sarah joined the Earl Hines band she not only shared vocal duties with Billy Eckstine but also played second piano to the leader. Few singers in jazz can have begun their professional careers so auspiciously, or so near the top. When Billy left to form his own big bebop band in 1944, Sarah went with him and was soon delighting her fellow musicians with her deft phrasing and musical daring. With this band she had some success with *I'll Wait And Pray* and she also recorded *Lover Man* with Dizzy Gillespie. During this period of her career she recorded *Time And Again* with the Stuff Smith Trio, and some excellent titles with small groups led by Teddy Wilson, which included such musicians as Charlie Ventura (ts) and Buck Clayton (tp). *September Song* received a delightful reading as did *When We're Alone* and *Time After Time*. For the most part, however, Sarah chose to work with modernists, including Tadd Dameron with whom she recorded fine versions of *If You Could See Me Now* and *I Can Make You Love Me*.

On these 1940s recordings her voice is a clear soprano but she had yet to develop the amazing range which makes her the most astonishingly endowed singer in jazz. Unusually among such singers, Sarah Vaughan's style is founded upon her prodigious technique which developed rapidly during the following years. A virtuoso singer, she is less concerned with the meaning of a lyric than with the accenting of a melody. The dazzling beauty of her voice singing variations on the melody is a thrilling object lesson in vocal control. The manner in which she swoops from octave to octave with precision and poise is little short of phenomenal. In performance she logically builds her interpretations, bringing them to an often surprising climax with a degree of musical daring few other jazz singers would even attempt. It is this astonishing range, timbre, eloquence and complete command which lifts Sarah Vaughan to the pinnacle shared by the greatest of jazz singers.

A 1955 album recorded with Clifford Brown (tp) and Paul Quinichette (ts) finds her in sparkling form on such songs as *Jim, Lullaby Of Birdland* and *I'm Glad There Is You*. Also in the 1950s she recorded two albums which provide perfect examples of Sassy's art: 'Sarah Vaughan at Mr Kelly's' and 'Sarah Vaughan After Hours at the London House'. Accompanied by small groups the creates a series of miniature classics with beautiful interpretations of *Detour Ahead, Three Little Words* and *You May Not Be An Angel*. On *Thanks For The Memory* she is strung up over the pronunciation of the word 'Parthenon' and has to restart the lyric twice. Backed by a subtle obbligato from Wendell Culley's muted trumpet, she then proceeds to build an admittedly flawed improvised classic out of what could have been a disaster in the hands of a lesser artist.

The 1950s brought Sarah an enormous popular hit with *Brokenhearted Melody*, and she also had great success with *Passing Strangers* and other duets she recorded with Billy Eckstine.

The vocal range Sarah had developed by this time was making her

Sarah Vaughan – astonishing virtuoso.

difficult to categorise, and also possibly a mite daunting to her accompanists. The dexterity with which she uses her voice (which many an opera singer envies for its range, power and superb texture) is quite remarkable and sometimes appears to demand a full orchestral backing. Yet, when accompanied by musicians as tastefully inventive as herself, she can turn in delightful and thoughtful jazz performances with just a handful of kindred spirits. *When Lights Are Low*, recorded in 1962 with Barney Kessel (g) and Joe Comfort (b) is one such example from many.

In 1977, recorded live at Ronnie Scott's in London, Sassy made a classic out of *Send In The Clowns*. In 1979 she turned her attention to the music of Duke Ellington on a memorable album recorded for Norman Granz which includes superbly inventive performances of *I Didn't Know About You* and *I Let A Song Go Out Of My Heart*.

On another album recorded for Granz, this time in 1982, Sarah was in a sole charge of her material, choice of accompanists and even designed the album sleeve. She also chose the album title but 'Crazy And Mixed Up' is the only untrue thing about it. Accompanied by Roland Hanna (p), Joe Pass (g), Andy Simkins (b) and Harold Jones (d) she performs a selection of superior popular songs. *I Didn't Know What Time It Was, Love Dance, You Are So Beautiful* are included, while on *Autumn Leaves* she gives a reading which can serve as a lesson for any singer in any genre.

Like Ella Fitzgerald, Carmen McRae (1922–) has successfully achieved the seamless blending of jazz with American popular song, but her work adheres more closely to the jazz idiom. Perhaps as a result of this her audience has long been much less than her talent justifies.

In the mid-1940s, she worked with the bands of Benny Carter, Mercer Ellington, Charlie Barnet and Count Basie, thus setting out on her career both contemporaneously and comparably with Sarah Vaughan. Like Sarah, Carmen McRae is also a gifted pianist and, at the time, was wholeheartedly involved in the new musical movement. She was also married to Kenny Clarke, the founder figure of modern jazz drumming. During these early years she played piano and sang around many of the New York clubs and rarely caught the attention of any but the local jazz enthusiasts and was certainly unknown so far as the wider audience was concerned. The work

Carmen McRae – uncompromising power.

served her well however, as did the spell she spent as intermission pianist at Minton's Playhouse in New York in the early 1950s.

Originally influenced by Sarah Vaughan and, above all, by Billie Holiday, who recorded one of her songs, *Dream Of Life*, in 1939, Carmen very quickly developed a powerful personal style to match her uncompromising personality. Nevertheless, she never lost her admiration for Billie and recorded an album, 'Lover Man', made up of songs associated with Lady Day.

Carmen has the ability to project a lyric with intimacy and warmth, and also with a turn of phrase which deflects the listener's attention from her relatively restricted vocal range. An intelligent singer, she has exceptional ability with ballads, singing them with reserve yet at the same time transmitting an aura of great emotional depth, as she demonstrates on *This Will Make You Laugh* and the old Ethel Waters hit *Suppertime*. Her relaxed and unpretentious phrasing is heard to great advantage on *Yardbird Suite* and *Our Love Is Here To Stay* from her excellent 'By Special Request' album recorded in the 1950s. This quality is also displayed on *A Beautiful Friendship* recorded at the 1979 Midem Festival.

At her best before a live audience to whom she can relate, Carmen McRae can be relied upon to mix sound standards with unhackneyed material. A typical set might include such ballads as *Body And Soul* but it may also have *Inside A Silent Tear*; while *On Green Dolphin Street* can provide an uncommon swinger alongside such old favourites as *Thou Swell*. An excellent example of a club date can be heard on the 1981 album 'Recorded Live at Bubba's', while a recent penchant for Latin American music can be heard on an excellent album she recorded with vibraphonist Cal Tjader shortly before his death in 1982.

The intrusion of private life – and private grief – into the work of several singers in the jazz and blues idiom will not have passed unnoticed. In the cases of Ella Fitzgerald, Sarah Vaughan and Carmen McRae, they have, for the most part, enjoyed some measure of stability and have led relatively uneventful lives outside their art. Of course, there have been ups and downs just as most people endure, but emotional crises have been either minor or, at least, have been kept well-hidden from public gaze. Not so with a lady who lived life to the limits and whose emotional upheavals can be heard in practically every note she ever sang.

Dinah Washington (1924–63) led a hectic life from the moment she was heard substituting for Billie Holiday at a Chicago nightspot in 1942. Dinah was born in Tuscaloosa, Alabama, but while she was still a child her family moved to Chicago. After winning a talent contest at the Regal Theater in the Windy City she took a job as ladies' room attendant at a local club. This was where she substituted for Billie. From there she auditioned for Lionel Hampton's band and worked with that powerhouse crew for three years until 1946. Two of her earliest recordings with the band were major successes for her: *Salty Papa Blues* and a song by jazz writer and occasional pianist and composer Leonard Feather, *Evil Gal Blues*.

During the mid-1940s Dinah embarked on several sessions in the rhythm-and-blues field and other successes were achieved, including *I Told You Yes I Do* and *Blow Top Blues*. More than any other singer of her era, Dinah Washington blended the sacred music of her childhood with the raunchy secularity of the rhythm-and-blues style, thus antedating the later boom in Soul music by a number of years. This style proved a potent force, especially in rural areas where *Ebony* magazine reported her being greeted with a religious fervour. Such acclaim sat uncomfortably with the unashamed worldliness she practised in her private life.

From the start of her professional career, Dinah had obviously made up her mind to enjoy her success. Jewelry, furs, cars, drink, drugs and men were what she spent her money on, not necessarily in that order and certainly with little discrimination. Several marriages resulted and countless liaisons. While a less strong-willed person might have faded under such high-living, Dinah's physical appearance gave every impression that she bloomed under it. The voice, however, tells another story.

Any singer, even one of little talent, can induce an impression of sadness; the ability to sing a 'tear' is not difficult. But the tear in Dinah's voice is very real and imparts to even inferior material a depth of emotion few other singers have achieved.

Her repertoire was extensive and she recorded hundreds of sides for various labels in all genres: the blues, rhythm-and-blues, jazz, popular songs of the day and of yesterday. All her material, good, bad and indifferent, improved with her reading of it.

Blue Gardenia, recorded in 1955 with Clark Terry (tp) and Paul Quinichette (ts) is a fine example of a lyrical ballad, while *Blue Skies*, from the previous year and recorded with a band including Eddie 'Lockjaw' Davis (ts) and Terry again, becomes an extended and definitive performance. In 1957 she recorded an album of songs written by or associated with Fats Waller, ranging from his early *Squeeze Me* to his late *Jitterbug Waltz*. On two songs from this album, *Honeysuckle Rose* and *Everybody Loves My Baby*, her husband at the time, Eddie Chamblee, puts down his tenor saxophone and sings very effective duets. These duets pre-echo Dinah's later hits recorded with Brook Benton: *A Rocking Good Way* and *Baby, You Got What It Takes*. Her choice of material from the popular standards was eclectic: Noel Coward's *Mad About The Boy*, Jerome Kern's *Smoke Gets In Your Eyes*, Cole Porter's *Ev'ry Time We Say Goodbye*, Duke Ellington's *It Should Happen To A Dream*, and she had an enormously successful hit with *September In The Rain*. To them all she brought conviction, eloquence and a sharply-defined assurance. Her handling of a lyric, often half-singing, half-speaking the words, was masterly as was her timing and always impeccable delivery.

She was also an accomplished musician and capable of playing several instruments. Her appearance at the 1958 Newport Jazz Festival, captured in the film *Jazz On A Summer's Day*, shows her commandeering Terry Gibbs' vibraphone for a brief foray which was far from amateurish.

Dinah was given the title 'Queen of the Blues' and certainly Alberta Hunter considered that at the time Dinah was the best blues singer around. This publicity tag was not as accurate as it might have been but, then, it would have been difficult to define precisely what it was she was queen of. Undoubtedly, she was always in total regal command of whatever she happened to be singing at any particular moment. On an album which used that same title, a strange collection of songs was gathered together with a mixture of accompaniments among which massed violins are well in evidence. The combination of doubtful material and overblown backing was enough to floor many a fine singer. Dinah tackled such songs as *More Than You Know*, *Ill Wind*, *Cottage For Sale* and, least likely of all, *Look To The Rainbow* with astonishing aplomb. Her voice slices through the accompanying meringue like a sharp but slightly jagged knife, in a manner which automatically relegates any other perform-

Dinah Washington – regal command.

ances of these songs to a very poor second place. In his sleeve note for Dinah's album 'The Jazz Sides', Dan Morgenstern perfectly expressed the relationship she had with other artists in her field, 'There are all kinds of singers. Somehow, Dinah made most of the others sound like little girls.'

More gifted than most, especially in her ability to imbue lyrics with special depths unflawed by the imprecise diction suffered by some of her contemporaries, Dinah Washington appeared to have everything going for her when the early 1960s Soul boom began. She could have been its queen without resorting to publicity agent's hype. Apparently settled in her private life with her seventh husband, she took a lethal combination of pills, almost certainly by accident induced through too much drinking. She was thirty-nine.

From the 1940s and on through succeeding decades, numerous stylish singers emerged and continued to bring to American popular song fine interpretations which fully demonstrated the influence of jazz upon themselves and their craft. Some have extended their reputations to the international market, others have remained little-known outside a relatively limited area. All display in varying degrees the influences of their predecessors and contemporaries in the field of jazz singing.

Barbara Lea, a superior and accomplished singer, displays similarities of style with Lee Wiley, handling the most difficult of lyrics in a relaxed and capable manner. Her version of Hoagy Carmichael's *Baltimore Oriole* is an especially fine example of her work. Good as Barbara Lea undoubtedly is, she could never compete successfully with her contemporary Teddi King. Teddi's finely controlled voice had a crystal-clear quality and was intimately expressive. Teddi's phrasing was both accurate and warm and she was perhaps the finest of the nightclub singers to emerge in the 1950s. She was only forty-eight when, in 1977, she died while working on what should have been her finest album. Consequently, she sings on only one side, the other side being completed by pianist Dave McKenna who was her accompanist on the date.

One of the most musical of singers, Helen Merrill is clearly concerned with the emotional potential in the lyrics of the songs she sings, often imbuing them with depths of passion that might well surprise their authors. Her version of *I Should Care*, recorded in 1968 with Dick Katz (p) Jim Hall (g), Ron Carter (b) and Elvin Jones (d) is a superb example while on Sigmund Romberg's *Lover Come Back To Me*, with the same musicians, plus Hubert Laws (fl) and a very expressive Thad Jones (tp) she swings lightly on a tune which was surely never meant for such treatment. This particular session, released as an album entitled 'A Shade of Difference' also includes an exquisite performance of *My Funny Valentine* on which the singer is accompanied only by Ron Carter's bass playing. It provides a lesson in lyric interpretation many better-known singers could do well to emulate.

Jane Harvey came into her own relatively late in her career and proved most impressive on her 'Fats Waller Revisited' album recorded with pianist Dick Wellstood. She had worked with Benny Goodman back in the mid-1940s, recording only very few titles, none of which demonstrated the qualities which emerged in her later work.

Carole Creveling and Lurlean Hunter sang well and displayed good phrasing; Corky Hale was pleasantly inoffensive; Beverley Kenney could swing and sang with some imagination; Mavis Rivers sang in a straightforward style and re-emerged in the 1980s to sing with the big band led by her son Matt Catingub.

Jerri Southern's intimate warmth is felt rather than heard. Her tasteful phrasing is used to good advantage on an up-tempo *It's De-Lovely* and a more reflective *I Hadn't Anyone Till You*. Sylvia Sims' husky and sensual voice was best heard on an album recorded with an orchestra directed by Ralph Burns on which she sang excellent versions of *My Ship* and *Down With Love*.

Julie London is another intimate singer with an agreeable sound, although her work is only on the edge of the jazz world. Similarly on the fringes was Jo Stafford, a tremendously popular singer in the 1950s whose vocal perfection was betrayed only by a certain lack of emotional depth in performance. Margaret Whiting is an exceptional stylist, latterly her sound closely approaching that of Ella Fitzgerald. Dinah Shore was another extremely popular singer who, while a pleasantly swinging interpreter, never quite got to grips with the jazz idiom. Dakota Staton's singing style, while modelled upon Sarah Vaughan and Dinah Washington, is highly mannered but she can certainly swing.

Ethel Ennis always demonstrated good diction and an understanding of the lyrics she performed. Technically, Alice Babs is a highly proficient singer with a broad range and her warm voice proved most suitable for her work with Ellington, especially on his sacred music. Morgana King is a fine classically-trained singer whose reputation is well-established among musicians but who has never quite fulfilled her potential in the eyes of the general public. Now that she has turned to acting (she played Brando's wife in the 1971 movie, *The Godfather*), it may well be that she will move permanently away from singing.

A fine pianist who recorded with Lionel Hampton back in the 1940s, Dardanelle Breckenridge continues the fine tradition of the cabaret singer but with considerably more jazz-influence than that demonstrated by some of her predecessors and contemporaries. In the mid-1980s she was delighting supperclub audiences in New York and recording more than ever before. Monica Zetterlund and Rita Reys were two of the more successful European singers to reach a wider audience.

The wide diversity of goals achievable by singers in jazz can be demonstrated by two artists whose paths crossed at a very early stage in their careers. The routes they then followed, and their place and status today, could hardly be more different.

In 1941 Benny Goodman was looking for a girl singer and auditioned several young hopefuls. One he summarily discounted as being completely unsuitable when she insisted on improvising on the melody in a way he did not like. Instead he hired Helen Forrest. About a year later, when Helen was leaving, he heard a young girl singing at the hotel where he was staying, liked her sound and hired her as replacement for Helen. The singer he had arbitrarily ignored was Anita O'Day; the singer he later hired was Peggy Lee.

Anita O'Day (1919–) has constantly demonstrated a powerful determination to do things her own way even if this led her along paths that were not merely dubious but also downright dangerous. She began her singing career while still very young, after a period spent surviving the Depression years as a marathon dancer. Always attuned to the rhythmic possibilities of music, her treatment of popular songs was necessarily unusual and met with little approval outside the jazz world. Her highly individual phrasing and her insistence upon reshaping songs to suit her somewhat limited range, led her to experiment at a time when such things were not done by many established singers, let along young upstarts no one had ever heard of. It was this attitude which doubtless led to the conflict with Benny Goodman.

Fortunately, at this same time Gene Krupa had heard Anita and had indicated that if his singer ever quit she could have the job. When Irene Daye eventually did leave Gene's band, Anita was hired and began a career that should have made her one of the biggest names in popular music today. Unfortunately, there were more than a handful of problems along the way, the gravest of which was fifteen years of addiction to heroin. Alongside this is a string of unsatisfactory and emotionally damaging relationships with men seem almost trivial. Eventually, following an accidental overdose which almost killed her (she was declared dead but her heart started beating again), Anita kicked the habit. Doing it alone, cold-turkey, was typical of a very tough-minded lady, whose determination can be heard in much of her work.

Anita then renewed her career and enjoyed greater success than ever before. By this time, however, times had moved on and she was past fifty. The really bigtime could no longer be hers but she set about the task of building upon her earlier promise and eventually consolidated her position as being one of the very best jazz singers around.

Back in the 1940s, when Anita joined Gene Krupa other changes were taking place in the band, one of which brought in trumpet player Roy Edridge. This was at a time when black musicians in otherwise all-white bands were almost non-existent but Roy proved a real boost to the Krupa band's sound and the numbers he performed with Anita became massive hits. These included *That's What You*

Think, Thanks For The Boogie Ride and, best-known of all, *Let Me Off Uptown* on which Anita's cry of 'Well, blow, Roy, blow' was picked up and echoed by wildly enthusiastic audiences. Her stint with the band did not begin quite so promisingly because Anita never matched the fans' image of what a band singer should sound like. Her intensely swinging performances were sung in a broken, Billie Holiday-inspired voice, which slurred across the melody to give a spontaneous swing quite unlike all other white band singers of the day. The dry, husky voice, with its limited range, allied to the hot and wailing beat she imparted, came to the fore with Krupa. It took time, but the fans were won over and, once they were, Anita became as big an attraction as the leader's extrovert drumming and Roy's fiery trumpet playing. Indeed, her popularity was such that after a while Roy became a little edgy and a rift developed. In fact, given the pressures on Roy as the only black man in the band, his displeasure was probably an expression of inner tension rather than a direct attack on Anita. Certainly, they later patched up any differences, real or imagined.

Despite her success with Krupa, singing with a big band was not to Anita's total satisfaction. The restriction imposed by the tight arrangements inhibited her freewheeling approach to jazz. In 1944 she joined the Stan Kenton band which must have proved even more stultifying, although they did have one big hit, *And Her Tears Flowed Like Wine*. For this, Anita asked for, and was allowed, a more swinging drummer than the band's regular man, which led to Jesse Price's temporarary stint with Kenton.

More than any other singer in jazz, Anita is musically closest to the drummer, the constant rhythmic interplay being aural evidence of this fact. Nevertheless, she has always displayed a marked involvement with her material which allows her to sing ballads with considerable intensity. A 1956 album, 'Anita', recorded with Barney Kessel (g) and others, found her in excellent form on *As Long As I Live, Who Cares?* and an uptempo *I'll See You In My Dreams*. Her interpretation of the Fats Waller-Andy Razaf tune *Honeysuckle Rose* on this date drew from the lyricist the comment that this was his favourite version.

At this point in her career, Anita was mostly working clubs and for the great majority of people, records were the only way they

Anita O'Day – independent individualist.

could hear her. All that changed in 1960 when the film *Jazz On A Summer's Day* was released. This allowed an international audience to hear and see Anita at the 1958 Newport Festival. As she admits in her revealing autobiography, she was stoned at the time, but few would have guessed from the effortless ease with which she swung through *Sweet Georgia Brown*, and a breakneck *Tea For Two* on which her interplay with drummer John Poole (with whom she has shared her most enduring personal relationship) is little short of miraculous. After this, offers of work flowed in but, as she was in the early years of her addiction to heroin, Anita was never able to build fully upon her potential. She continued working throughout the hard times, and it is difficult to determine any real lack of quality in her performances. The problems took their shape elsewhere, but not in her appearance. In the 1959 movie, *The Gene Krupa Story*, she played herself fifteen or more years younger and managed to look the right age. She has since made other movie appearances, sometimes singing, other times in an acting role. Nor did her recordings display her problems.

On a 1961 album of music associated with Billie Holiday, 'Travellin' Light', she made no attempt to sing like Billie but nevertheless conveyed the emotional bonds she obviously felt. (Although, as she recalls in her book, her meetings with Billie were never cordial, despite their once shooting-up together.) In the late 1960s, when Anita's habit became critical and she also suffered heart failure, she set about the task of straightening out her life with characteristic grit. Her later recordings, many of which were from live concerts in Tokyo and San Francisco, display a gifted jazz singer at the very height of her powers. Fortunately, the quality of Anita's voice was never an essential part of her performance. Rather, it was what she did with this limited asset that counted. This has meant that the passage of time, which eventually erodes all voices, has not damaged her career as much as it has those of many other singers.

Whether singing such uptempo swingers as *You're The Top* or ballads like *I'll See You In My Dreams* she demonstrates a striking honesty of approach which makes her instantly identifiable and classifiable as a jazz singer of extraordinary merit.

Benny Goodman demanded perfection in everyone, not least in himself. It is not surprising therefore that he was less than happy

Peggy Lee – perfect confidentiality.

with the self-assured young Anita O'Day who was determined to do things her own way. In Peggy Lee he found a much more malleable personality, and one who was no less a perfectionist than himself.

Peggy Lee (1922–) brought to the band a voice that was not only different in character to that of Anita, it was different to that of any other big band singer of the era. The voice was, and remains, softly limpid with no sign of exertion, regardless of the volume of the accompaniment.

The striking contrast between band and voice was apparent from the first record she made, *Elmer's Tune*, which became a big hit. Other records succeeded rapidly: *My Old Flame, How Deep Is The Ocean* and the massively successful *Why Don't You Do Right?* By the time she left Goodman in 1943, to take on a solo career, Peggy Lee's assurance of success was virtually guaranteed. An accomplished musician, she was already writing some of her own material (sometimes in collaboration with her then husband, guitarist Dave Barbour) and many proved to be huge sellers. They included *It's A Good Day, Mañana* and *I Don't Know Enough About You* (and she later worked on the score of the Walt Disney movie *Lady And The Tramp*). Her performance of *Lover* was also quite outstanding and was a deserved popular success.

Although her range is narrow, she never appears to strain beyond its limits. There is an intense degree of confidentiality in her singing style, which proves enormously attractive on love songs and the more sentimental ballads, and adds a strangely persuasive element to the uptempo swingers which she also favours. Her highly successful 1950s albums included a superlative set on 'Black Coffee' which included the title song, an elegant *Easy Living*, a relaxed *Gee, Baby Ain't I Good To You*, and a lightly swinging *I Didn't Know What Time It Was*. 'Dream Street' is a supreme example of a well-planned, constructed and performed album and, as such, proved to be a total artistic and commercial success.

By this time, Peggy Lee's audience appeal had stepped far outside the confines of the jazz world and she never looked back, despite several illnesses which left her dependent upon a portable oxygen tent. Quite clearly, she is not happy at improvising, preferring instead to work on carefully prepared material. The perfectionism which so appealed to Benny Goodman persists through to the present day, with as much attention being paid to the lighting, her appearance, and the outward accoutrements which have become the accepted perquisites of a major star – suitable transport, hotel accomodation and the like. A Peggy Lee show and, indeed, every song in it, are productions – and rarely, if ever, show any variation. It is in this last respect that Peggy Lee's later career moved her furthest from the jazz world. Yet in the vocal inflections apparent in all her best work, her jazz origins are clear and, indeed, have proved of positive help in overcoming some of her latterday problems with pitching.

Among the singers whose careers have paralleled those of Peggy Lee and Anita O'Day is Rosemary Clooney, who worked with the Tony Pastor band before going solo. Rosie displays a mature and effective style which she combines with sensitive phrasing. For a long time she was involved with the more popular areas of singing. Her duets with Bing Crosby proved enormously successful as did such hits as *Come On-a My House*. Nevertheless, she is at her best when teamed with sympathetic jazzmen. Illness kept her profile low in recent years but she is now back to form and enjoying a resurgence in her career, thanks in part to many fine recordings she has made on the West Coast.

Helyne Stewart is a versatile singer with a strong voice who has never received the attention she deserves. Marilyn Moore recorded an excellent album in the late 1950s on which she almost succeeded in recreating the sound of Billie Holiday. Since then her career appears to have ended, which is unfortunate because, despite the strong element of impersonation in that album, many fine attributes were clearly apparent. Teresa Brewer graduated from a straight popular artist to performing very creditably on an album of Bessie Smith songs recorded with Count Basie's band. Carol Sloane has a mellow voice which she uses with intelligence and charm.

Then there is Betty Bennett who originally intended to be an opera singer but was introduced by her mother to the music of Ellington and Basie. Betty learned her trade touring with the Alvino Rey band and, in 1949, was hired by Charlie Ventura to replace Jackie Cain and Roy Kral. In addition to singing solos, she also used her voice instrumentally with the band, thus gaining invaluable grounding. While with Ventura she became increasingly aware of the lyrics, until then having concentrated principally upon her jazz sound. Betty has a flexible and sincere style with good diction and control and sings with great natural charm and intelligence. She is now retired from singing but remains active in music and is married to Mundell Lowe the guitarist and musical director of the Monterey Jazz Festival where their 1975 wedding took place.

But what of the men? Although they are certainly outnumbered by women, among the jazz-influenced song stylists are a number of male singers whose credentials are most impressive.

Mel Tormé (1925–) first came to wide public attention when he sang with the Artie Shaw band in the 1940s and had a hit with *What Is This Thing Called Love* on which he was joined by the vocal group, the Mel-tones. Nicknamed 'The Velvet Fog', which accurately conveys an impression of his vocal sound, Tormé was a precocious child who proved adept at various musical instruments before concentrating upon singing. One of the few 'musician's singers' to gain equal popularity with audiences, Tormé's control, pitching and diction are virtually perfect. Like Crosby and Sinatra before him, he is not strictly a jazz singer but of the three is the most jazz-orientated. With considerable skill he has contrived to blend the best qualities of the hip singer with those of the stylists, while never losing sight or sound of his jazz roots.

Among his best-known songs are *Mountain Greenery* and *A Christmas Song*. The latter is one of his own compositions and is, perhaps, the best of its kind.

In recent years, Tormé has worked extensively with pianist George Shearing and many technically brilliant performances have resulted. The emotional depth and the jazz content of their interplay is less striking but cannot detract from the astonishing extent of their musical empathy.

Other male singers include Jackie Paris who worked on 52nd Street in the 1940s and also toured with Charlie Parker. He knows the value of a good lyric and sings with subtlety and considerable jazz feeling. Johnny Hartman is an underrated singer of exceptional quality. The jazz-tinged singing of David Allyn is enhanced by his good pitch and diction, and he and Matt Dennis appeal to the fringe audience attuned to the work of Sinatra. Bill Henderson's work is unusually tasteful and well conceived. He has a personal style which

150

Mel Tormé – technically brilliant.

combines the warm intimate tone of Nat Cole with the urgent delivery of Joe Williams.

Mark Murphy (1932–) comes from a highly musical family and began an extensive round of touring and recording in the 1950s. An excellent album from the early 1960s is 'Rah' on which his instrumentally-conceived singing style is clearly defined. This period also brought him great popularity in Europe to which he regularly returns for club engagements. He has cited Lee Wiley and Peggy Lee as influences but there are certain similarities of style which link him to Tormé.

Murphy's repertoire, which he draws from such diverse sources as Jon Hendricks and Joe Turner, is sung with great dexterity and with evident good humour. The breadth of his repertoire allows him to appeal equally to the general audience and to the more selective jazz crowd.

From the mid-1970s onwards he recorded several superior albums on which his material is both unusual and eclectic and his performances well-nigh flawless. Ably backed by good modern jazzmen, including Randy Brecker (tp), Mike Brecker (ts) and David Sanborn (as) on a 1975 album, 'Mark Murphy Sings', and by Richie Cole (as), Slide Hampton (tb), Ronnie Cuber (bars) and others on 'Satisfaction Guaranteed' in 1979, he ranges through all moods from the blues to the best of contemporary popular song with even a passing nod at the stylistic effects of rhythm-and-blues along the way.

A highly accomplished singer who has never enjoyed the wide success he deserves, Mark Murphy has recently displayed an interest in the music of Latin America which he sings with considerable jazz feeling.

While no one would argue against the inclusion of Nat 'King' Cole (1917–65) in any account of jazz piano playing (he forms the stylistic bridge between Art Tatum and Oscar Peterson), as a singer he is generally disregarded. In the early 1940s, as a piano-playing leader of a popular supperclub trio in Los Angeles, Cole began singing an occasional song. He found that his huskily intimate voice appealed to the public and was easily persuaded to expand his singing at the expense of his piano playing. He had several hit records, including *Route 66* and *Straighten Up And Fly Right*. In time, he moved well away from the jazz world but in many of his later performances, such

Mark Murphy – highly accomplished.

Nat Cole – huskily intimate.

as *Let There Be Love* with George Shearing and 'Welcome to the Club', an album he recorded with a Count-less Basie band, he demonstrates considerable feeling for the jazz idiom. However, the blues were not his métier, as evidenced by a generally unsatisfactory album brought out to accompany his starring role as W.C. Handy in the 1958 movie *St Louis Blues*.

Nat Cole influenced numerous singers, including such diverse talents as Ray Charles and Johnny Mathis, and even inspired pianist Oscar Peterson to record an album of songs in similar style, but few of his successors worked within the jazz field.

Cole's contemporaries during his Los Angeles days were a different matter, however, for that particular scene in the 1940s proved to be a highly significant staging post in the development of jazz-influenced popular music in America.

5 *Shake, Rattle and Soul*

Although the term 'rhythm-and-blues' was not immediately applied, this musical form was essentially intact in the midst of the Swing Era. Its most noticable early flourishing was in Los Angeles in the early 1940s where more mixing of black and white audiences took place than in most other parts of the nation. This had its effect upon the nature of the music which eventually emerged.

Rhythm-and-blues drew its staple ingredients from various areas of jazz and the blues. From jazz it took the relentless, driving rhythms of boogie-woogie and the flashier elements of the concurrent jump bands; from the blues it took many technical devices but not usually the twelve-bar structure, favouring instead 8- and 16-bar formats. Like the blues it was an essentially vocal music. It contained the fervour of gospel music and the earthiness of black ghetto life and, at its best, it swung madly.

If anyone noticed that the term, rhythm-and-blues, soon shortened to r&b, was an inoffensive version of the tags, like 'ebony', 'coloured', 'race' and 'sepia', attached by record companies to black music in the past, no one appeared to care! Important for the companies and their artists was the fact that after the end of World War 2, the market for records among black Americans ceased to be regional and became national instead. Demand was consequently massive and the record companies responded to it. Among the enormous number of musicians swept along on the r&b tide were

156

(*Top*) Louis Jordan, Wynonie Harris, Jimmy Witherspoon; (*below left*) Big Maybelle; (*below right*) Big Miller.

many whose background – church choir and/or childhood vocal group preceding a move into a professional singing career – closely resembled that of people of an earlier day who became blues singers.

The outstanding exponent of this musical form in the immediate post-war years, and the closest to the jazz world both in background and performance, was Louis Jordan (1908–75). Jordan played alto saxophone in various minor bands before joining Chick Webb in 1936. Outside of working for Ellington or Basie, this was one of the top jobs for a black musician in the Swing Era, and if this was a good place for Jordan the instrumentalist to be, it was also an excellent vantage point from which to observe the making of a singer – Ella Fitzgerald. But Jordan the singer developed in a very different manner to the shy, withdrawn young woman.

After his two-year stint with Webb, Jordan became linked with the jump band tradition which had emerged along New York's 52nd

Street during the late 1930s. The driving, rhythmic pulse of such bands was a direct predecessor of the r&b bands of the 1940s. The combination of the tight, crisply swinging instrumental sound and Jordan's engagingly extrovert stage presence promised success. What confirmed that success in national terms, however, was Jordan's singing style which appealed equally to black and to white audiences. He was a sophisticated urbanite and it showed. He was also a witty man with an endless fund of humorous lyrics – many of which touched upon the old staples, drugs, sex and booze. Of course, such subjects were nothing new in blues-related singing but with Jordan it all came out as good, clean fun – well, almost.

Jordan's first big hit was *Choo Choo Ch'Boogie* in 1942 and he was still capable of producing a massive hit a decade on with his 1951 success, *Saturday Night Fish Fry*. Only a handful of his songs were in the traditional blues repertoire: *I'm Gonna Move To The Outskirts Of Town* was one. For the most part he concentrated upon comedy numbers: *Five Guys Named Moe, Ain't Nobody Here But Us Chickens* and *Open the Door, Richard*, and on other popular songs of the day that were definitely light-hearted: *Is You Is Or Is You Ain't My Baby, Knock Me a Kiss* and *Caldonia*. Less successful were Jordan's occasional forays into Caribbean-flavoured music. *Run Joe*, a calypso, did not work, although his 1945 recording with Ella Fitzgerald of *Cold Stone Dead In The Market* was highly popular.

In the 1960s, Jordan toured Britain, playing with Chris Barber's band, and entertained his audiences with undimmed enthusiasm. The enthusiasm was still shining brightly in 1974 when he was recorded at a club date in California.

This new form of American popular music which Jordan and his contemporaries heralded was felt by many to be far removed from jazz. True, some of his successors have at best only tenuous links with jazz. (In the case of Bill Haley, even tenuous might be too strong a word.) Jordan's connection with jazz was far stronger, although it is understandable if the fact that he was always obviously having fun has led to him being discounted from serious consideration as a jazzman. Understandable but unfair, for in Jordan's work there is always an important strain of jazz and the blues. If, as the title of one of the hits expressed it, he usually *Let The Good Times Roll*, it came at a time when jazz needed an injection of fun to help

WEST GLAMORGAN
COUNTY
LIBRARIES

boost it through a particularly sticky patch in its history.

Following hard on Jordan's heels came a seemingly endless succession of r&b singers, many of whom moved into the burgeoning rock 'n' roll movement in the 1950s. In reality, when deejay-record producer Alan Freed applied the term rock 'n' roll to black r&b it was part of an exercise, at first unconscious, which turned the music from being black for black audiences into black for white audiences. Later, and inevitably given the exigencies of the record industry, it became white music for white audiences, but by then the character of the music had altered irrevocably. Of course, some singers did retain, for a time at least, strong elements of the jazz and blues content of r&b. Singers like Joe Turner and Helen Humes did so, and their successful invasion of this new territory made it even harder than before to pigeon-hole their work.

Measured by a commercial yardstick, the most successful of the post-Jordan r&b singers were those who were able to adapt, as he had, to the mixed Los Angeles audience. For the most part, the white elements therein wanted a smoother style that was seemingly more sophisticated (at least by their measure of such things). Black audiences were divided: some wanted the gloss of supposed sophistication; others, possibly intuitively, realised that the apparent rawness of early r&b was its lifeblood. This was reflected in the importance attached to the music at a time when a new sense of freedom pervaded urban black communities, even if they were still largely confined to inner-city ghettos. Music was just one way, but a way that was accessible to all, in which blacks could declare their new post-war identity.

Nevertheless, r&b was picked up by the young white audience, albeit for different reasons. This audience wanted something radically different to the music their parents had enjoyed. Swing was old hat, bebop was not 'popular music', so they picked up on the new, urgent sounds of contemporary black music. The already urbanised blues that had developed elsewhere, especially in and around Chicago, in earlier decades, offered possibilities but it had to be changed. To effect that change new musicians came along.

Among the post-Jordan singers whose work retains the strongest elements of jazz and blues are Charles Brown, Roy Brown, Wynonie Harris, Roy Milton and Amos Milburn.

159

As was apparent from the early career of Nat Cole, the music scene in Los Angeles had a highly sophisticated facet. As Charlie Gillett has recounted, supper-club diners and drinkers liked their music soft so as not to disturb their conversation. Trios were the ideal size group and they abounded in the LA area.

Nat Cole was the main attraction, but when he moved on to national and international fame, the top spot locally was filled by The Three Blazers. This was a band formed by guitarist Johnny Moore (whose brother Oscar played guitar with Cole) and included pianist-singer Charles Brown.

Despite his early training as a pianist, Charles Brown (1920–) entered a career as a teacher of chemistry. In 1943, by then living in Los Angeles, he decided on a change in career having already discovered he could earn better money moonlighting as a club pianist. In 1944, as a member of The Three Blazers, he also began singing regularly. The fame of The Three Blazers spread and in 1946, thanks to being signed up by the William Morris Agency, they were headliners in New York and a hit at the Apollo Theatre. The trio made some successful records but they split up in 1948 with Moore continuing to use the group's name.

Charles Brown was now not only on his own but was virtually unknown by name. Starting from scratch, but, fortunately, with a recording contract as a solo artist, he soon achieved popularity. He had a string of successes through into the early 1950s: *Trouble Blues*, *My Baby's Gone*, *Black Night* and *Hard Times*. In the late 1950s he recorded successfully with Fats Domino: *I'll Always Be In Love With You* and *Please Believe Me*, thus extending his career beyond the point at which the r&b boom faded, unlike many others who declined with it. The principal reason for this was that, like Nat Cole, Brown had a soft, smooth voice which admirably fitted the new mood for sentimental ballads, often performed with strings and heavenly choirs, with which the older generation of music lovers sought to stave off the worst effects of too much exposure to rock.

Brown's singing style, which was modelled on that of Pha Terrell, is delicately balanced between the softer end of the late r&b scene and the saccharine-sweetness of the contemporary popular field. Unlike Cole, Brown retained a blues flavour to his singing (accurately defining himself as a 'blue ballad singer') and there was certainly a hard edge to his performance, echoing the earlier styles of Leroy Carr and Lonnie Johnson. This hard edge gave credence to the feeling of disillusion which pervades much of Brown's work, a disillusionment which predates his decline in popularity.

By the end of the 1960s, Brown was on the edge of obscurity but a 1976 appearance at the San Francisco Blues Festival showed he still had what it takes. He is still active in the 1980s, singing in LA clubs now to audiences who are there not to be heard but to hear him.

Roy Brown's singing blended the extremes of gospel, emotionally-charged solemnity and joyous exhortation, and drew many fans in the 1950s. In many respects his style moved away from the secular r&b field, predating the important movement of black music of the next decade. He had hits with *Good Rocking Tonight* in 1947 and, six years later, *Laughing But Crying*.

Wynonie Harris (1915–69) sang in his hometown of Omaha, Nebraska, for a while before moving to Los Angeles. After a spell singing with the Lucky Millinder band, during which he recorded *Who Threw The Whiskey In The Well*, he went solo as an r&b singer just as rock 'n' roll was making its first stirrings. He had limited success with *Bloodshot Eyes* and *Good Rocking Tonight* but audience tastes were changing and, although he could adapt technically, the young did not want him, preferring singers from their own age group.

Harris sang the blues in a jumping, extrovert manner which displayed a mixture of influences, including Joe Turner, Louis Jordan and T-Bone Walker. Essentially an urban blues singer, he worked with many fine jazz musicians: Illinois Jacquet (ts), Charles Mingus (b), Jack McVea (as, ts) and Teddy Buckner (tp) among them. His mid-1940s recordings with men like these produced many fine performances: *Wynonie's Blues, Young Man's Blues, Somebody's Changed The Lock On My Door*, all of which show a man with a well-developed sense of the blues tradition who was sadly underemployed during his unfortunately shortened career. When times changed and he could not work, he dropped out for a while, made one unsuccessful attempt to return, but a further attempt was denied him when he fell victim to throat cancer. His son is Wesley Devereaux, a popular singer with a strong feeling for the blues.

Roy Milton hailed from Tulsa, Oklahoma, and like many others sang in the church choir before going on the road as a singer – with the Ernie Fields band. In 1938 he took up residence in Los Angeles and when r&b came in he had a local base on which to build his career. He made his first records in 1945 and had a hit with *R.M. Blues*. Highly successful into the mid-1950s, Milton's popularity waned in the face of the rock 'n' roll onslaught.

Amos Milburn came to Los Angeles from Texas with Lightnin' Hopkins; he stayed and did well with his first record, *My Baby's Boogying*, in 1946. It was the following year, however, when he recorded *Chicken Shack Boogie*, that he had a major hit. An accomplished, hard-hitting boogie-woogie piano player, Milburn's career mirrored Roy Milton's in that his successes were followed by decline when rock 'n' roll came in.

As his nickname suggests, Ivory Joe Hunter was also a pianist. Although he recorded in the r&b idiom he was often accompanied by out-and-out jazzmen. Not one to settle for second best when the best were available, he recorded with Ellingtonians Harold Baker (tp), Tyree Glenn (tb) and Russell Procope (as, cl) on *Siesta With Sonny* and *Send Me Pretty Mama*; with Johnny Hodges (as) on *I Quit My Pretty Mama*, while Taft Jordan (tp) and Budd Johnson (ts) played on *S.P. Blues*.

Cecil Gant was another good boogie-woogie pianist and first attracted attention in 1944 while still in the army (he was billed as 'Pvt. Cecil Gant, the G.I. Sing-Sation'). Occasionally backed by jazzmen, Wingy Manone for one, he had a string of minor hit records through the late 1940s but never had a chance to capitalise on these before his early death. His most popular recording was *I Wonder*.

The 1950s and 1960s saw a resurgence of interest in the blues. The older generation of blues singers were the first to spark interest in a new generation of audiences. They included Lonnie Johnson, Big Bill Broonzy, Sonny Terry and Brownie McGhee, while Josh White enjoyed marked success in Britain where his emotionally intense performances were often seen on TV. Then, gradually at first, the modern Chicago blues-style singers came to the fore.

Some of the earlier songs of Muddy Waters (1915–) had enjoyed limited success. In the 1960s, however, he received an unexpected fillip to his career. Tours of Britain turned some young British singers on to his vocal style. Prominent among them was Mick Jagger of The Rolling Stones and this prompted a new audience to listen. They liked what they heard and Waters' career blossomed. Among the successful records he made were *Rollin' Stone* and *Hoochie Coochie Man*.

The playing and singing of Robert Johnson was reflected in the music of Elmore James who, in his turn, influenced a younger generation of bluesmen. His singing had about it an air of dramatic tension. His best known record was *Dust My Broom*. Jimmy Reed, an overly casual and incoherent singer, somehow projected his highly original personality to considerable success. Curtis Jones was an undistinguished if pleasant singer. J.B. Lenoir sang his blues in an unusually light, high-pitched voice.

Chester Burnett was an uncompromisingly original performer, marking his singing with a distinctive sound effect which earned him his nickname: Howling Wolf. A well-developed sense of drama pervaded his live performances and his best-known recordings capture some measure of this: *I Ain't Superstitious*, *Smokestack Lightning*, *Back Door Man*, *The Red Rooster*, and many more.

Aside from the innumerable Chicago-based singers were others, many having been around for some time, who also enjoyed new acclaim.

Of these it is Aaron 'T-Bone' Walker (1913–75) who is the most complete performer. Essentially a leading exponent of urban blues, his penchant for playing his guitar over his head or behind his back led casual observers to suspect that his playing was all flash and glitter. Nothing could be further from the truth. An excellent blues shouter in the true Texan tradition, Walker was at ease with both jazz and blues standards and was very influential both as singer and instrumentalist. He was equipped with the facility for studding his material with intriguing phrases and he consistently demonstrated his ability to give the gaudier side of r&b a solid core of genuine blues feeling. His 1940s recordings, many of them his own compositions, reflect this side of his work: *Mean Old World*, *First Love Blues*, *Stormy Monday* and *T-Bone Jumps Again* demonstrate his ability at its peak. A few years on, his voice beginning to flake, he still performed ably on *Evenin'* with apparently unlikely but highly effective accompaniment from Dizzy Gillespie (tp) and Zoot Sims (ts).

José Antonio
·HOLLYWOOD·

T-Bone Walker –
leading bluesman.

He even chanced his arm and recorded with The Sweet Inspirations (a female chorus) and a Hollywood-style string orchestra.

Listening to such recordings it is hard to equate this performer with the youth who made his first records (*Trinity River Blues* and *Wichita Falls Blues*) when known by the somewhat exotic handle of Oak Cliff T-Bone. But that young country blues singer did mature into the later urban bluesman and r&b exponent, although it is doubtful if his audiences in the 1940s, 1950s and later were either aware of or in tune with his background.

As a child, Lightnin' Hopkins learned from Blind Lemon Jefferson, and Texas Alexander to whom he was related. Working in Los Angeles in the 1940s, alongside the growing r&b movement, Hopkins retained his basic style and regaled his listeners with cogent observations on the contemporary scene. He had hit records in the 1950s with *Hello Central* and *Coffee Blues*.

164

Much more attuned to the new white rock 'n' roll scene of the 1950s was Chuck Berry (1926–) who began recording in 1955, by which time r&b was fast being swamped. His *Roll Over, Beethoven* and *Too Much Monkey Business* were strongly influenced by the blues. As the decade wore on he became more obviously at ease with the requirements of rock 'n' roll and became a leading black exponent of the form, along with Fats Domino, Little Richard and Tommy Tucker, a pianist-singer who had some success in the pop world with *Hi-Heel Sneakers* but was at heart a good blues performer.

B.B. King (1925–) is the most successful and influential of the latterday blues artists. His performances, both as singer and as guitarist, have influenced such performers as Freddie King, Bobby Bland and Albert King. He has a strong voice in the blues shouter tradition; his own influences go back to Lonnie Johnson, Lowell Fulson and T-Bone Walker, and he can be interestingly compared with Muddy Waters. Unlike Waters, King concentrated upon a more melodic sound, preferring the lyrical qualities of the blues. It is this quality which has opened up his work to the wider audience but, until the later stages of his career, when he became an international star, his repertoire was always heavily blues orientated. Exceptional among numerous recordings is his album 'Live at the Regal' from 1964, which includes *Sweet Little Angel*, *Every Day* and *Woke Up This Mornin'*.

Other male singers who have worked in the r&b tradition include Percy Mayfield, a sophisticated modern blues singer, equally at home with a big band or with a small blues combo. His biggest hit was *Please Send Me Someone To Love*. Bull Moose Jackson was a rather florid-toned blues and ballad singer who turned in good performances on the bawdier songs, such as *Big-Legged Woman*. Clarence 'Gatemouth' Brown is a good blues guitarist and singer whose recent career has seen him entering the somewhat more lucrative field of Country and Western music.

Although known primarily as a guitar-playing bluesman, Lowell Fulson sings well in the tradition of T-Bone Walker. His style does bear strong reflections of the Kansas City shouters, undoubtedly a result of the time he spent with such bands as those led by Jay McShann and Buster Smith. Mercy Dee Walton, an articulate modern blues singer had a major hit with *One Room Country Shack*.

Although the r&b scene was male-dominated, there were good female exponents as Helen Humes' career has indicated. They included Savannah Churchill, Ruth Brown, Etta James, Ella Johnson, LaVern Baker and Wynona Carr.

Savannah Churchill began her recording career somewhat belatedly in 1943 with Benny Carter. She became one of the earliest r&b singers to gain success in the 1940s and appeared at the London Palladium in 1951. Some of her most jazz-influenced recordings were made in 1944. On *You're Gonna Change Your Mind* the influence of singers as diverse as Lil Green and Maxine Sullivan is clearly heard. *Teasin' Me, Two-Faced Man* and *Fat Meat Is Good Meat* offer good examples of her rhythmic style. Her career was abruptly halted in 1956 when she was struck by a drunk falling off the balcony at a Brooklyn club. Resulting ill-health forced her into retirement shortly afterwards.

Ruth Brown (1938–) came from a musical background (her father was director of a choir in Portsmouth, Virginia) and she sang briefly with Lucky Millinder's band. When Blanche Calloway heard Ruth she took her to New York where in a few years she established a reputation with a small but enthusiastic following. A record in 1953, *Mama, He Treats Your Daughter Mean*, a 16-bar blues, was a minor hit, and under Blanche Calloway's management she enjoyed some success. A poised singer with considerable swing, Ruth's r&b career did not isolate her from the jazz world and she recorded with the Thad Jones-Mel Lewis big band.

Ruth's voice has a richness akin to Dinah Washington's, who was her major influence, but without the same density of sound or that deep sadness. Let Ruth loose on a bouncy treatment of *Yes, Sir That's My Baby* and *everyone* has fun. Even on songs like *Trouble In Mind, Be Anything But Be Mine* or *Black Coffee* the mood is lightened by her lyrical interpretation. On unlikely material which brings Al Jolson to mind – *Sonny Boy* and *Bye Bye Blackbird* – she overcomes the dangers of sentimentality and banality with her simple *joie de vivre*. Her rocking enthusiasm on *I'm Gonna Move To The Outskirts Of Town*, on which she is accompanied by Jerome Richardson or on *Fine Brown Frame*, which swings more than the famous Nellie Lutcher version, suggests that this is the best kind of material for her. Yet she is highly effective on her versions of *It Could Happen To You* and *I Can Dream, Can't I?*. Undoubtedly, Ruth Brown's vocal style and talent deserves a much wider audience than has been the case.

Etta James enjoyed an early success with *The Wallflower* which made it into the rock 'n' roll charts in 1951. From time to time she has varied her repertoire with more overtly gospel-style singing. *Something's Got A Hold On Me* and other songs, complete with choir and organ accompaniment, are designed as church rafter raisers. Her voice is occasionally strident but when faced with material obviously aimed at the popular market, say, *I Worry About You*, she deliberately softens her sound. Her recordings in 1953 for the Modern label tend to be simpler and more direct than her later records for Chess. Shuffle rhythms keep things moving along and the piano is much more preferable to the later organ. The honking tenor saxophone is merely fashionable dressing without which some r&b and rock 'n' roll singers, or, at least, their producers, seemed unable to get along. Her songs of this period include *Roll With Me Henry* and *If It Ain't One Thing*, which today sound mildly risible thanks to a 'doo-wop' female backing group.

Ella Johnson sang with the band led by her brother Buddy but despite numerous recordings between 1939 and 1951, most of which were distinctly above average and very popular with the black audience, she remained obscure, little heard, and is all but forgotten today. A great individualist, especially when working with material arranged by her brother, her best-known song is *Please, Mr Johnson*, recorded in 1940. This song lives on, often with the name changed to allow singers to involve their own accompanist in the lyric. Anna Mae Winborn, who led the Sweethearts of Rhythm, sang in a very similar blues style, as did Tiny Davis.

Chicago-born LaVern Baker worked the clubs in the 1940s and 1950s, touring Europe in 1953. The following year she had hits with *Tweedle Dee* and *Jim Dandy* which eased her over the dividing line between r&b and rock 'n' roll, thus limiting interest in LaVern's career for jazz fans, although she did record an excellent album of Bessie Smith numbers with jazz accompaniment. The strong blues feeling she displays might well have given her a different kind of appeal but she would probably have met with less commercial success. Through the 1950s and 1960s she had a string of hits but failed to gain the enormous popularity which attended emerging singers like Dionne Warwick.

Wholly immersed in the blues was Willie Mae 'Big Mama' Thornton (1926–84) who had a big round-toned voice with a great feeling for the idiom. She occasionally worked with r&b bands, including Roy Milton's, but was much more at home with the blues. A large lady who could and frequently did put the fear of God into any accompanist who strayed into her territory, she had several successes, including *Sweet Little Angel* and *Hound Dog*, both of which she sang at John Hammond's 1967 'Spirituals to Swing' thirtieth Anniversary Concert. Also in the 1960s, she toured Europe and was recorded in Germany and England, the results being among the best blues records of the decade. In the 1980s, approaching death through cancer, and a frail shadow of her former self, she was televised preparing for and appearing at a concert. Clad in clothes she had worn when still living up to her name, Big Mama looked pathetically comical until she began to sing. She had to perform seated but the strength of her voice still echoed the majesty of her youth and her main influences, Ma Rainey and Bessie Smith.

Mabel 'Big Maybelle' Smith was another powerful, tough singer whose fierce declamatory delivery gave her blues an urgently violent edge.

Among other ladies are Esther Phillips, an r&b graduate who developed a quiet jazz style based upon Billie Holiday and who met with some success before her untimely death. Koko Taylor is a powerful singer whose first success came in 1963 with *Honkey Tonkey* and she has continued to impress in the Chicago-based blues field which, a handful of stalwart ladies to the contrary, tends, like the r&b field, to be heavily male dominated.

The r&b singers of the 1950s, whatever their quality, extended enormous influence upon innumerable younger artists (some of whom were already establishing themselves). Some of these youngsters had talent, others needed (and obtained) hyping. Predominantly white, and surprising to some observers of the time, often non-American, these young singers adapted, changed and adulterated rhythm-and-blues until the new term, rock 'n' roll, was needed to differentiate them and their music from the rougher-hewn black originators. In time, rock 'n' roll came to mean more than merely music. Just as the Jazz Age was a term which spread outside the immediate, implied musical definition, so rock was applied to the generation brought up to its sounds. Apart from the music, rock conveyed attitudes towards politics, economics, lifestyles, dress and behaviour.

Heading the white American rockers, and most influential, was Elvis Presley while Jerry Lee Lewis, Bill Haley and countless others had their followings. It is beyond the scope of this book to explore this field and these artists, nevertheless, the black influence (of, say, Otis Blackwell on Presley) is apparent to all but the most blinkered observer. In Great Britain the dominant figures were, of course, The Beatles, while The Rolling Stones proved very nearly as popular and even longer lasting. The Stones, and their contemporaries The Animals, adhered more closely to the black origins of their style than did the Beatles and most other groups of the Swinging Sixties. In such small respects, the British rock 'n' roll singers cleaved closer to the earlier r&b tradition, but in jazz terms the connection had dissolved.

Of all the musical forms touched upon so far, the two seemingly least likely to prove compatible, let alone to prove suitable for blending into a new whole, are rhythm-and-blues and gospel singing. Yet, blend they did and the form which emerged became hugely popular through the 1960s and into the following decade. By the mid-1980s, this new hybrid was one of the most visible and readily accessible forms of singing in the Afro-American tradition. The form is, of course, Soul.

The line connecting gospel to spirituals and early hymn-singing in the slave states of the American South in the nineteenth century is distinct but it is not easy to differentiate readily between the various manifestations this form of singing has taken.

Undoubtedly, early religious music in the South captured a fervour usually missing from that of European communities, although it must be stressed that this was not a quality produced solely by black interpreters. White fundamentalist religion in the Deep South also carried its own peculiar vocal fervour, although how much this is a result of cross-fertilisation with black song is open to speculation. A form of singing which displays similar root qualities to spirituals can be found in British folk-psalmody. As musical historian John Storm Roberts has suggested, this form of religious singing, which was highly popular in seventeenth-century Europe, became similarly popular during the next century in the New World.

Although blacks in eighteenth-century America sang psalms, they turned to hymn-singing at the beginning of the nineteenth century when a great religious revival took place. Known as the Second Awakening, this drew together many thousands at interracial camp meetings. The manner in which blacks performed hymns met a developing desire among white fundamentalists who were seeking to break away from the old religious traditions. Spontaneous creation of new religious songs occurred, thus compensating for the fact that most of the congregations, black and white, were illiterate. The term 'spiritual songs' had been in use for many years but now was used specifically to denote this new kind of music.

In 1871, a group of singers from Fisk University in Nashville, Tennessee, went on a tour of the north. The tour went on and on, crossing the ocean to Europe and by the time the Fisk Jubilee Singers returned home in 1878 the spiritual had, in David Ewen's words, 'captured the heart of the world'. Yet, the Fisks had compromised. As Viv Broughton has commented, they 'were the first, but certainly not the last, black American artists who dressed up the image and dressed down the music in order to cross over to the white market'. Indeed, to cite Broughton again, the Fisks themselves were quick to reassure the genteel churchgoers who flocked to hear them that they had 'purged the songs of all ungainly africanism'.

The compelling power of words and music in the spirituals render it entirely unsurprising that, despite changes in emphasis and function caused by the passage of time, which led to the more emotional and dramatic gospel song, this particular musical form has continued to make itself heard through to the present day. Although for some black Americans the spirituals carry unwanted echoes of past times when their forebears were cruelly oppressed, they also carry a message as valid today as at the time of their emergence. As historian John White has suggested, the spirituals, however interpreted, 'speak as much to the cruelties inflicted on as to the resistance displayed by American slaves. That they also gave to the world a vivid and compelling amalgam of words, images and music is one of the more bitter ironies of Afro-American history.'

The religious songs of early slaves, shaped as they were by the white European hymn tradition, and actively encouraged by slaveholders, were unusual in form. Unlike many traditional forms of song, the Negro spiritual, as it became known, was designed for group performance. Essential to it were the harmonies evolved by its performers. Generally absent were solo singers although a leader was often necessary for the call-and-response structure of some spirituals. This is very similar to the form employed in the work song. David Ewen suggests two further categories of spiritual. In one, solo singers can have a more dominant role. This is the sorrow song which, with its stately grandeur, became popular with audiences much wider than those usually associated with religious singing. The other form taken by the spiritual is that of the catchy, rhythmic, syncopated melodies which lent themselves admirably to gospel music when interest in black religious music blossomed in the 1950s.

Another important factor was that despite its religious origins, the spiritual and especially gospel song, is undoubtedly caught between the sacred and the secular. In John White's words, it is at once 'other-wordly and this-wordly, passive and protesting'. This occasionally uneasy mixture can be personifed through the career and the music of Thomas A. Dorsey.

The life and career of Thomas A. Dorsey (1899–) have all the makings of a Sunday School version of a Horatio Alger story. Born in Atlanta, Georgia, in his early years he lived the high life among the lowlifes and earned a living of sorts as a blues singer. Photographs of him at this time, when he was known as 'Georgia Tom', reveal a sharp dresser with all the slickness of a man who would feel most at home in any big city bawdy house.

Later, after he turned to God (or, rather, back to God for his father was a preacher) Dorsey revealed a hitherto unsuspected side to his character and became the most influential composer and male performer of gospel.

In his early recordings his voice is light and displays a lilting awareness of the humour inherent in much blues material. He was a member of Ma Rainey's Georgia band in the early-1920s, having previously worked as a part-time musician, playing piano and singing whenever he could and spending some time with Les Hite's band in Chicago.

While with Ma Rainey, Georgia Tom struck up a working relationship with Tampa Red and their duo recordings display a noticably lighter-hearted approach to the blues than is apparent in the work of many of their contemporaries.

Despite Georgia Tom's relatively humorous view of the blues, when he began writing and performing gospel songs in the early-1930s he was able to imbue them with an earthiness few other male gospel singers achieved, while never deliberately coarsening his vocal sound. He also brought to his work sophisticated musical skills, doubtless sharpened as a result of his studies at Chicago's College of Composition and Arranging.

In old age, Thomas A. Dorsey could still inspire an audience in a place of worship although, as the extraordinary film *Say Amen, Somebody* demonstrates, by 1982 much of the congregation's fervour was self-induced for the singer's voice had gone.

It would be facile to use one man's life as a continuing thread through the complexities of black music in America, yet in the case of Georgia Tom Dorsey it is decidedly tempting. With his *Mississippi Bottom Blues* he is the country blues singer, the vaudevillean on *The Doctor's Blues*, an urban bluesman with *Rollin' Mill Blues*, and then the gospel singer *par excellence* on innumerable songs, many of which he wrote himself. His best-known and loved gospel compositions are *Take My Hand, Precious Lord* and *Peace In The Valley* (a song which Elvis Presley made into a million-seller).

A gifted composer and an excellent performer, Georgia Tom Dorsey's chosen career through later life has wrongly removed him from the front rank of blues singers, a place his earlier work more than justifies.

Like Tom Dorsey, the career of Sister Rosetta Tharpe (1921–73) covered two distinct yet linked areas of black music. In the early 1940s she spent a year singing with the Lucky Millinder band and proved a remarkable asset as several best-selling records indicate.

(*Top*) Rosetta Tharpe – powerfully rhythmic; (*below left*) The Clara Ward Sisters; (*below right*) Mahalia Jackson – faultless command.

These include *I Want A Tall Skinny Papa* and an excellent *Trouble In Mind*. This venture into the underworld of jazz appeared to affect her conscience and she was soon safe in the bosom of the church, rocking congregations into ecstasy with her passionate, almost frenzied singing. Her work demonstrates the powerfully rhythmic form some gospel song takes and her duets with Marie Knight (herself a vigorously swinging singer) are among the classic jazz-influenced gospel songs. As a gospel singer, Sister Rosetta Tharpe, like Dorsey, was able to enhance the fabric of her sacred perform-ances through her wide experience of secular singing.

Another gospel singer of note was Clara Ward (1924–73) a lady who became one of the most revered of her kind, whether singing alone or with the Clara Ward Singers. The group's animated passion and dedicated fervour is extremely moving and can be heard to

173

advantage on such songs as *Hold Back The Tears* and *I'm Goin' Home*. While still a child, Clara attracted a great deal of attention; in later years, partly through her powerful, impassioned singing but also through her bizarre taste in clothes, and especially hats, she and her followers became as eye-catching as they were vocally impressive.

Marion Williams also became immensely popular both as a solo singer and as a member of Alex Bradford's group. Their 'Black Nativity' show was instrumental in the development of interest in gospel music in Britain in the 1960s, thanks to tours and television appearances. Accompanying Bradford and Marion Williams were Princess Stewart, a sombre figure who sang with a controlled but seemingly bottomless contralto, and the Stars of Faith, a version of the Clara Ward Singers.

Of all the gospel singers, prime place must be granted to Mahalia Jackson (1911–72) whose majestic voice and presence impressed audiences throughout the world. As a child, Mahalia, who was born in New Orleans, sang in the gospel church where her father was pastor. Although her chosen path was as different as could be, she always readily acknowledged the influence of Bessie Smith and Mamie Smith. In her mid-teens, now living and working in Chicago, she continued to sing in church and as a member of a gospel group. Invited to make records in the 1940s, she unexpectedly found herself with a million-selling hit. This was *Move On Up A Little Higher* and it launched her on a hugely successful career.

Mahalia Jackson's repertoire was predominantly sacred and even the few non-sacred songs she sang were imbued with her deep-seated personal beliefs. Her faultless command and deeply-etched sincerity are heard on countless recordings. She reached an audience of millions, thanks both to these records and to her appearance in the film, *Jazz On A Summer's Day*. In this she sang *His Eye Is On The Sparrow*, *It Don't Cost Very Much* and *Walk Over God's Heaven* which represent some of the finest moments in all gospel. The closing scenes of the film, when she sings *The Lord's Prayer*, are remembered by all who have been and heard it, regardless of any personal religious conviction.

Mahalia's early material was directed at the black audience but as time passed her appeal broadened until she was attracting a predominantly white audience. Some felt that she simultaneously lost touch with blacks and she was criticised for this, criticism which was fuelled by the fact that success also brought her great wealth. But, regardless of her financial rewards and the composition of her audience, none could seriously doubt that Mahalia's heart was always with her God and she never lost the power to move people. At the 1963 March on Washington she stood beside Martin Luther King Jr and sang Thomas A. Dorsey's *Take My Hand, Precious Lord* to an audience numbering a quarter of a million. (It was one of King's colleagues, W. Herbert Brewster, who composed Mahalia's hit, *Move On Up A Little Higher*.) Following King's assassination in Memphis in 1968 Mahalia sang *Precious Lord* at the funeral and the same song was sung at her own funeral, this time by Aretha Franklin.

The sacred music of such performers as Mahalia Jackson blends persuasively with the blues in the work of artists like Odetta Gordon (1930–). Indeed, she is so strongly blues-orientated that to classify her as a gospel singer is inaccurate and unfair, as she has worked very successfully with Count Basie and Buck Clayton, and has appeared at numerous jazz, blues and folk festivals. A singer of power and integrity, Odetta's decision to follow a varied career should have drawn her a much wider audience than has been the case. Certainly, her talent deserves more recognition.

The sacred music of the gospel singers and the blues feeling in much of it, when allied to such rhythmically engaging songs as *He's Got The Whole World In His Hands, Oh, Happy Day* and *Take This Hammer* attracted the attention and interest of the rhythm-and-blues artists. It was when they took such songs and reproduced them in their own secular style that Soul emerged to become the dominant form of black music in the 1960s.

One of the most influential Soul singers of the period was Ray Charles (1930–) who was a well-tutored musician as a very small child. His formal progress was hampered by the loss of his eyesight at the age of seven but, fortunately, Charles was a determined individual. He discovered within himself a steely spirit which allowed him to overcome not only this handicap but also to take on racism and prejudice and even to fight successfully against hard drug addiction.

Although strongly influenced by gospel singing, Ray Charles was also a follower of blues-balladeer Charles Brown and achieved his first success in show business singing in a style modelled closely upon Nat Cole. The addition to his repertoire of songs from the hotter end of the gospel range and some of the currently popular blues heralded the emergence of a distinctive singing style. Charles' popularity developed through the 1950s and on into the early 1960s, but he was restricted by the strongly r&b-orientated nature of the record company he was with at the time. A change to a new label in the early 1960s allowed him to expand his repertoire and, almost at once, his audience similarly expanded to encompass not only blacks but whites.

His first major success for the new label was Hoagy Carmichael's *Georgia On My Mind* and this was swiftly followed by a continuing string of hits: *I Can't Stop Loving You, What'd I Say, Hallelujah I Love Her So, You Are My Sunshine, Hit The Road, Jack,* and *Busted.* All were sung in a hoarse, declamatory style which, allied to a deeply emotional feeling, imbues his obviously secular material with the fervour gospel singers bring to their religious music. This and his urgently rhythmic delivery have made Ray Charles instantly identifiable and hugely popular the world over. These popular successes have obscured his ability to bring to his material a strong feeling for the blues.

While r&b had been noticably the preserve of male singers, and gospel largely the domain of the ladies, it was appropriate therefore that their offspring, Soul, had excellent practitioners of both sexes.

In addition to Ray Charles, James Brown, Bobby Bland, Jackie Wilson and Sam Cooke all had major successes, bringing to their work distinctive overtones of their own earlier musical preferences. Among the ladies were some of the r&b stars who adapted successfully, and several talented newcomers, among whom Aretha Franklin proved to be one of the most successful, and also one of the best.

Born in Memphis, Aretha Franklin (1942–) was raised in Detroit where her father was a popular, dynamic evangelist. Aretha was greatly influenced by Mahalia Jackson and Clara Ward, both of whom visited her father's church and her home. Her early career was only moderately successful but a change in record companies provided an upturn. Oddly enough, while Ray Charles had benefited

Aretha Franklin – impassioned power.

by leaving Atlantic it was Aretha's arrival at this company that boosted her career. This was in 1966, some six years after her recording debut. Her first record for the new company, *I Never Loved A Man*, sold over a million copies, and the following year she successfully toured Europe. Despite mismanagement of her career, Aretha has enjoyed considerable and consistent success with regular nominations for Grammy Awards.

Aretha displayed a personal style and maturity from a very early age. Known as The Queen of Soul, she exhibits great versatility and variety in performance, moving effortlessly from smooth lyricism to impassioned power, and all with considerable feeling.

Other female singers for whom Soul provided an important ingredient in their careers include Della Reece, a successful cabaret artist who has a richly powerful voice but, despite her influence by Dinah Washington, sings with little subtlety. Similar in style to Reece is Gloria Lynne who has a big but rather nasal voice. Nina Simone can be bizarre and overdramatic but at her best is a poised and musicianly vocalist. Amanda Ambrose sings in a manner reminiscent of Simone and is heard to advantage on uptempo numbers. Nancy Wilson is best regarded as a superior singer of popular songs who displays the influence of Dinah Washington but can be over-stylised in her delivery. Natalie Cole, who is the daughter of Nat Cole, is an effective singer, with stronger evidence of gospel in her style than most. Tina Turner's gospel-originated style, with its screams and whoops, is rasped out with force but little subtlety.

A product of Berry Gordy's Tamla-Motown recording empire is Diana Ross who gained great success during the 1960s as a singer of songs which, while not Soul, always had soul. In 1971 Diana scored a personal triumph when she played the part of Billie Holiday in the Motown movie, *Lady Sings The Blues*. Although Billie's life was grossly distorted and the film as a whole was no tribute to the greatest singer in jazz, Diana Ross's singing was substantially more than adequate. Without falling into the trap of trying to sound like Billie, she adopted jazz inflections and sufficiently adjusted her own style to divert any criticism from herself – even from those who had gone along to scoff. Indeed, the changes effected by Diana for this movie, stayed with her for some years.

In recent years the popular music scene has undergone innumerable shifts in emphasis but there has been no marked innovation and neither have there been any innovators. However, there has been an encouraging expansion in the number of singers whose careers bear the hallmarks of jazz singing, either through deliberate intent, as displayed by Diana Ross, or through osmosis. This form of learning from the past has been achieved in part through listening to records, and also through the opportunity many have had to listen to some of the old survivors.

This combination – the tough, old singers of yesteryear who have lingered on, those in middle-age whose styles have remained unchanged despite events around them, and the young newcomers eager to pick up the best (and occasionaly the worst) of their elders – has helped to build a jazz scene which is as vibrant today as at any time in its past.

It is to these singers: young, mature and old, black and white, traditional, mainstream, modern and avant-garde, that the jazz audience can now turn for a continuation of the story and development of jazz singing.

6 Survivors, Keepers of the Flame and Bebop Betty

The seeds of the flourishing jazz world of the mid-1980s were planted at various points in the previous quarter-century, even in the days when it looked as if a permanent blight lay over the land of jazz.

Singers of quality abounded in the late 1950s and have featured prominently in jazz in each succeeding decade. Most encouraging, and probably instrumental in the relative strength of jazz today, is the fact that no one pocket of jazz had the edge. The blues had its practitioners, old and new; the Dixieland revival had its moments; the jazz mainstream has had a veritable flood of quality talent; the modern end of the jazz spectrum also had its rising, and sustaining stars; and there has never been any shortage of up-and-coming youngsters eager to test the possibilities of a career in jazz, an always doubtful proposition even in the best of times.

The blues enjoyed a revival which has persisted through to the present day. Recordings by those who had died, or were alive but no longer able to sing, came into vogue and Bessie Smith's true status as 'Empress of the Blues' became apparent to audiences far removed from those who had known or heard her in person back in the 1930s. A Broadway show, 'Me and Bessie' starring Linda Hopkins, celebrated her as did an excellent biography by Chris Albertson, and Bessie's unmarked grave at last acquired a headstone, thanks in part to the efforts of rock singer Janis Joplin.

Still around and able to enjoy the revival of interest in the blues was Alberta Hunter. As recounted earlier, she had dropped out of singing in the 1950s and for many years made a career in nursing. Forced to retire from nursing in 1977 because of her age, she was then past eighty, she was invited to sing at Barney Josephson's club, The Cookery, and was a great success. From then until her death in 1984 she appeared regularly at the club, made TV and concert appearances, began recording again, and wrote the score for the motion picture, *Remember My Name* (1978). Among her old compositions used in the score, and which she performed on the soundtrack, were: her theme, *My Castle's Rockin'*; her classic *Down Hearted Blues*; and *The Love I Have For You* which, in particular, proved not to have dated at all and was still a supremely effective ballad. In one of her TV shows, recorded at the Smithsonian Institute in Washington DC she showed that her voice was still in remarkably good condition and her ability to control an audience was quite astonishing. It was a demonstration which gave some indication of the power and authority exerted by the old-time blues singers over their audiences. In many of the songs from her extensive repertoire, she also displayed a sharp wit and a subtle way with a risqué lyric.

The blues revival threw up an occasional curiosity, such as intermittent appearances by Mama Yancey (1896–), widow of the fine boogie-woogie pianist Jimmy Yancey. She began making records again when in her eighties and her shrill, unprofessional singing offers an unsophisticated, back-parlour kind of blues few latterday performers, let alone their audiences, have heard.

A much more sophisticated blues artist of comparable vintage is Eva Taylor, who had worked in Sissle and Blake's 'Shuffle Along' on Broadway in 1921, had married composer Clarence Williams, and recorded with Louis Armstrong in the 1920s. She turned up in Sweden, in 1976, to record with local musicians. As recounted earlier, Sippie Wallace was another survivor who opened ears and kept the flash-bulbs popping at the Nice Jazz Festival in 1982. Two other elderly vocalists who rarely left their home town of New Orleans but continued to perform were Billie Pierce, a raw blues singer who worked with her husband, trumpeter Dee Dee Pierce, and pianist Sweet Emma Barrett.

The revival of interest in jazz and the blues in the 1950s was by no means an exclusively American phenomenon. Jazz flourished in most countries with Great Britain being particularly inundated with countless traditional bands which helped split the country's fans into traditionalists and moderns (or, as the quaint phraseology of the day had it, mouldy fygges and dirty boppers).

The American singers who struggled through the somewhat repetitious repertoire of the Dixieland bands included Claire Austin who had a deep and pleasant voice, occasionally subject to uncertain pitching. Claire is one of the few white singers in the blues tradition who bears comparison with her black counterparts. Her usually effortless style belied the fact that her career was constantly interrupted through enforced absences from the business when she sought other work as a means of ensuring survival. In a 1954 session with a band led by veteran New Orleans trombonist Kid Ory she displays the effect enforced lay-offs could have. Although her voice is in good shape, there is a marked absence of enthusiasm for the occasion.

Barbara Dane also benefited from the boom and made a number of interesting records. Better known as a folk-singer, her 'Living with the Blues' album, recorded in 1959 with Earl Hines, showed her as a competent performer of commercially-slanted blues songs.

Then there was the unaffected Clancy Hayes, a harmlessly jolly singer in the minstrel tradition who was, nevertheless, highly popular with traditional enthusiasts.

In Britain, almost every trad band leader took on singing chores in a kind of musical version of *droit du seigneur* which ended in the vocal rape of many an unsuspecting lyric. Fortunately, one or two leaders displayed more acumen. Notable among these was Chris Barber who brought over a succession of fine American singers to tour with his band: Big Bill Broonzy, Sister Rosetta Tharpe, Sonny Terry and Brownie McGhee, Muddy Waters and Louis Jordan. Largely as a result of Barber's efforts, British and European audiences had an opportunity to hear and admire singers of high quality and the appreciation of the blues in Britain swelled to unexpected and long-lasting proportions.

The Barber band's own singer was Ottilie Patterson who provided a pastiche of the classic Bessie Smith style and, as a result, was markedly better than most revival singers. Beryl Bryden was another singer whose extrovert personality gained her many admiring fans in Britain and Europe.

One singer from the British trad era who survived long past the boom years was George Melly (1926–). After working with the Mick Mulligan band, Melly retired to a calmer life and became an art critic. In 1971, he returned to singing and has since toured extensively with John Chilton's Feetwarmers, playing concerts and clubs, making TV and radio appearances, and has recorded several albums. In the best sense of the term he is at heart a vaudevillean with a great sense of fun and boundless enthusiasm for his material, which helps overcome any shortcomings he may have as a singer.

That curious desire of bandleaders and instrumentalists to sing has been a persistent feature of jazz on both sides of the Atlantic for many years and has had decidedly variable results. Among these musicians have been Woody Herman, Zoot Sims, Jimmy Rowles, Buddy Rich and Chet Baker.

Central to the blues tradition was the rediscovery of many artists of a bygone era, thus offering a taste of the real thing rather than the artificial flavouring of their well-meaning followers.

Peter Chatman (1915–) was born in Memphis, Tennessee, and took the name of his birthplace around the world through his billing as Memphis Slim. He had enjoyed a highly successful early career including a spell as Bill Broonzy's pianist. As a piano player, Memphis Slim is reminiscent of Roosevelt Sykes; as a singer he demonstrated a considerable degree of originality. Later, picking up the mantle following Broonzy's death, he became enormously popular in France and Britain where he still tours. Some of his latterday performances have tended to become pale reflections of his own earlier style. A 1961 recording session with a small, shouting band produced fine performances of *Let The Good Times Roll, Creole, It's Been Too Long* and *I'm Lost Without You*, and to some extent echoed an even more successful recording from a few years earlier, which produced the album 'At the Gate of Horn'.

Since the 1960s Memphis Slim's output has been extensive but not always well-judged, for example a questionable blues, *If You See Kay, (F.U.C.K.)*. A duo album with Willie Dixon was pleasant stuff but stretched neither players nor listeners; a London-recorded set with Alexis Korner showed skill but little of the emotional depth of which the singer is capable; a session recorded in Copenhagen with home-grown accompanists was simply bland. If he failed to stretch himself in later years, and often resorted to evocations of other (sometimes lesser) bluesmen, to the younger-generation audiences Memphis Slim became the epitome of the old-time country bluesman. In reality, and when caught at his considerable best, he is a fine urban bluesman whose country roots give added texture to his performances. His compositions include *Beer-Drinking Woman, Blues Is Everywhere* and *Everyday I Have The Blues*, all of which he played and recorded many times.

Champion Jack Dupree (1910–) was born in New Orleans, learned to play the piano and eventually became a vaudeville entertainer, working in harness with Ophelia Hoy. If Champion Jack's piano playing was inclined to be erratic, his singing always had a rugged charm. (His nickname stemmed from youthful forays as a prize-fighter.) His material and delivery often employed vaudeville techniques, investing many songs with uncouth humour and wry observation. He spent several years in Europe, residing for a time in Yorkshire, England.

Curtis Jones resurfaced after many years in the wilderness. Cousin Joe Pleasants is another barrelhouse bluesman, still carrying the story of the blues forward to further generations. Kate Webster also continues the blues tradition. Pianist and singer Connie Berry worked in Harlem and on 52nd Street in the late 1930s, where for a time she was a member of the Spirits of Rhythm. Back in the limelight in the early 1980s, she recorded a fine album, 'Wouldja For A Big Red Apple', singing to her own accompaniment such songs as *'Tain't Nobody's Biz-ness If I Do* and Lil Hardin Armstrong's *Brown Gal*.

But the old-stagers did not have it all to do. Many young singers emerged whose adherence to the blues line helped guarantee that the tradition would live on through means other than records.

Important among these is Carrie Smith (1941–) who was born in Georgia and, like so many other blues singers, began singing in church. Her family moved to New Jersey and, while working in a factory there, Carrie was hired as a maid by singer-actress Juanita Hall. Learning that her new employee could sing a little, Miss Hall encouraged her and soon Carrie was performing professionally. This was at the start of the 1970s and she quickly developed a localised reputation and, more importantly, became known and respected by musicians. Carrie has acknowledged her debt to Bessie Smith and Dinah Washington whom she regards as her prime influences, although she also greatly admires the work of Billie Holiday. Still relatively little known, even to jazz audiences, Carrie Smith is only one of countless singers in the history of jazz and the blues who deserve a wider audience.

Her recording of Ben Harney's *You've Been A Good Old Wagon But You Done Broke Down* from the 1974 Carnegie Hall concert by the New York Jazz Repertory Orchestra is excellent as is the strutting *Cake Walking Babies From Home* recorded on the same date. For too long these two titles were her only available recordings. Things then began to change a little.

Carrie's overt espousal of the music of Bessie Smith in no way limits her repertoire: *All Of Me, Don't Be That Way* and *I Cried For You* all received excellent interpretations on a 1976 Paris session on which she was ably accompanied by Doc Cheatham (tp), Vic Dickenson (tb) and Eddie Barefield (cl). The success of this and another album she made in Europe around the same time led to a 1978 New York date which was also decidedly eclectic. Backed by Art Farmer on flugelhorn, with Budd Johnson playing tenor saxophone and also responsible for the arrangements, Carrie turned in a splendidly rowdy *When I've Been Drinking* which rubbed congenial shoulders with elegant versions of Billy Strayhorn's *Lush Life* and the old Eubie Blake-Andy Razaf song, *Memories Of You*.

Jeanne Carroll, another singer with an attractive, blues style, worked with Little Brother Montgomery in the 1960s. Nancy Harrow had a musical voice and displayed a real understanding of the basics of jazz. She made a big impression with one record album but little was done to build upon this. Olive Brown is an exuberant singer in the vaudeville tradition, thus being one of the few ladies around to keep this particular flame burning. Amina Claudine Myers is difficult to categorise; on a 1980 album she devoted one side to the music of Bessie Smith which she sang in an effortless bluesy fashion without any serious attempt to evoke the Empress's sombre majesty, while on the other side she sang a powerful extended piece entitled *African Blues* which drew its inspiration from the very roots of Afro-American music.

Etta Jones is another singer who has made a substantial mark in recent years. She had recorded some interesting sides in the mid-1940s with various bands which featured fine jazzmen. On *Salty Papa Blues* and *Evil Gal Blues*, cover versions of Dinah Washington's first records, Etta was accompanied by Barney Bigard (cl) and Leonard Feather (p) while on *Blues To End All Blues, Mean To Me, Ain't No Hurry Baby* and *The Richest Guy In The Graveyard* she was backed by Buck Clayton (tp), Flip Phillips (ts) and Johnny Guarnieri (p).

After years in comparative obscurity, Etta returned to the scene in the mid-1970s and from this moment on was frequently accompanied by the fine Texan tenor-saxophonist Houston Person. Her 1976 record sessions find her using such traditional material as *Exactly Like You* but *Second Time Around* and *You'd Better Love Me*, show her at ease with quality popular songs. Her 1978 recordings with Houston Person show a balanced use of her technique. These sessions include standards of an earlier period which have long been a staple part of the jazz singer's repertoire: *What A Little Moonlight Can Do, Ghost Of A Chance, I'm In The Mood For Love* and *Ain't Misbehavin'*, although Etta was always prepared to tackle the potentially maudlin, imbuing it with the kind of sharpness employed by Billie Holiday and Dinah Washington. Etta Jones enjoyed a major triumph at the 1984 Nice Jazz Festival.

More readily associated with the mainstream of jazz, and owing clear debts to the major stylists, are a group of singers, mostly but not exclusively American, in whom the jazz tradition not only lives on but positively flourishes.

Susannah McCorkle is one of the most stylish and technically gifted American singers to emerge in recent years. Her polished performance is displayed at its best when she performs superior popular songs. On two such albums she was accompanied by some fine British jazz musicians led by her husband, pianist Keith Ingham. This was in 1976 and 1977 and the albums, which were built on the work of Harry Warren and Johnny Mercer respectively, ably demonstrate that a good tune and a meaningful lyric are meat and drink to her. In an interview conducted by Brian Priestley for 'Jazz Journal International' Susannah and Anita O'Day discussed other singers and their own approach to singing. Not surprisingly, Anita's comments were lucid and pointed; for those who were unfamiliar with Susannah McCorkle and her work, she too proved to be a perceptive and highly articulate lady whose talents are lamentably underused on both sides of the Atlantic.

Sue Raney displays a happily varied range of songs on her album 'Ridin' High' on which she teamed up with some of the best LA-based jazzmen. After all these years and thousands of performances, it is quite a feat for a singer to succeed as she does in breathing new life into Hoagy Carmichael's *Stardust*. Lisa Rich is a stylish singer with an unusually wide repertoire which draws on lesser-known songs by such jazzmen as Dave Frishberg and Chick Corea, Beatles songs and even folk-music from Central Europe. New York songstress Marlene Ver Planck uses her perfectly pitched, lilting voice to good account, stylishly vocalising against jazz-tinged arrangements.

Lorez Alexandria began as a gospel singer and studied formally in Chicago before beginning work in the clubs of her hometown. She sang with pianist Ramsey Lewis in the late 1950s before moving to Los Angeles in 1961 where she continued working clubs and on TV. Her 1978 album 'A Woman Knows' contains many excellent examples of her work, including a performance of *I Can't Get Started* that is so good it puts into the shade just about every other version ever recorded.

Lorez has a deep, burnished voice and sings superbly, whether on ballads, which she favours, or on lithely swinging tunes. Her version of *Harlem Butterfly*, the title song of a 1984 album, is exquisite. Clearly, she has learned from the past mistresses of jazz singing, but she has absorbed and redefined so that, stylistically, she is her own woman. Perhaps her only failing is a preoccupation with vocal tricks but, this apart, she is a gifted singer.

Marva Josie is a pleasant, forceful singer whose years with Earl Hines brought her to a wider audience than most of her contemporaries. Dee Dee Bridgewater has a fine, flexible voice and her repertoire ranges over the whole spectrum of jazz and the blues, with occasional forays into popular song. She constantly displays an

187

inventiveness which sets her apart from most singers of her generation but, like so many such artists, record companies seem determined to keep her from the general public. Vi Redd is one of the growing band of fine female jazz instrumentalists who are at last beginning to make deserved inroads into the supposedly all-male environs of the jazz world. In addition to playing booting tenor saxophone she also sings with good intonation and phrasing. Astrud Gilberto has a small, childlike delivery and sings in the Latin American idiom which has little to do with the true jazz traditions. She is most known for her recording of *The Girl From Ipanema* on which she was accompanied by tenor saxophonist Stan Getz.

The low-key approach to her work displayed by Sheila Landis has kept her from the wider public, despite an appealing freshness. Anne Marie Moss paid her dues with the Maynard Ferguson big band and displays a wide yet discriminating choice in songs. Lilian Terry is also discriminating, and she concentrates upon drawing all she can from the lyrics of her material.

Jeannie Lambe is a good British singer, often found working London clubs with her husband, tenor saxophonist Danny Moss. Pug Horton is a relatively unknown singer who came to wider notice in 1978, following her marriage to saxophonist Bob Wilber. She sings well with enthusiam but has yet to develop an individual style and sound. Barbara Jay is another British singer whose work is little heard outside the London club scene where she works with her husband, tenor saxophonist Tommy Whittle. Also British is Joan Efford who works in Los Angeles with her husband, tenor saxophonist Bob Efford.

Another American is Marian Montgomery, who sings in a warm, Southern-accented voice. She has had a sporadic recording career. Occasional records filtered out of America in the early 1960s and a few have been made in Britain in more recent years, especially following upon attention paid to her by the non-jazz press when she began collaborating with classical pianist-composer Richard Rodney Bennett. A tantalisingly elusive singer, Marian Montgomery's infrequent appearances on national radio or TV make it difficult to keep track of her development, but when she does pop up there is usually something in her performance to interest the jazz audience.

Shirley Horn works mainly in Europe and continues the tradition of the singing pianist. A tasteful singer, she consistently demonstrates great style. Betty Comora is a stylish cabaret singer who also occasionally plays concerts. Her repertoire draws upon the more traditional aspects of jazz: *Hard-Hearted Hannah*, *Pete Kelly's Blues* and the popular songs of the past several decades. Claire Frazier has made a substantial impact upon European audiences, thanks to her successful appearance at the 1982 Nice Jazz Festival.

Ernestine Anderson worked with several powerhouse bands in the late 1940s, including Lionel Hampton's, but first gained recognition in Sweden, thanks to a successful album recorded there in the mid-1950s. This was 'Hot Cargo' and for some years thereafter Ernestine found herself better known and more popular in Europe and resided in London for a while. Through the 1970s, however, she lived and worked in Los Angeles and made several excellent albums, always backed by the best of jazzmen.

Equally at ease on ballads – *Days Of Wine And Roses* and *Am I Blue*, and on uptempo swingers – *Take The A Train* and T-Bone Walker's *Stormy Monday*, Ernestine always displays superb timing and a deep sense of the meaning of a lyric, while never allowing the words to overrule her awareness of the importance of the jazz content of her material. She is one of many singers whose qualities are instantly apparent even to the casual listener, which makes the fact that she is relatively unknown outside the jazz world even more frustrating, and sad, than usual.

An American singer who made an impact on the British scene in the 1960s was Joy Marshall. Following Joy's tragically early death, her contemporary Salena Jones continued to exploit successfully the fringe market.

Few singers in jazz have the range of Cleo Laine who uses her multi-octave voice to great effect. One moment she is singing with crystal-like clarity in her highest register, next comes a throaty growling some four octaves lower. Married to alto saxophonist John Dankworth, her recent career has been linked with decidedly non-jazz performances and much of her time and effort, like her husband's, is dedicated to their musical education establishment at Wavendon in England. For the jazz enthusiast, some of Cleo Laine's best work dates from the early 1960s with the second Dankworth band.

One of the best of a number of singers to emerge from Scandinavia is Norwegian-born Karin Krog. She has a clear voice with a good range and excellent taste in the selection of her material, all of which she sings effortlessly and with great swing. In recent years she has added to her repertoire from the work of Dave Frishberg, placing his material alongside popular standards – *Jeepers Creepers* and *Love Walked In*, old jazz classics *I'm Coming Virginia*, and jazz works of a more modern flavour, such as Tadd Dameron's *Trane*.

Also from Norway is Laila Dalseth who lacks the polish Krog's greater experience has provided but is clearly a singer of promise.

The men are a little thin on the ground in the mainstream of contemporary jazz singing but there is Joe Lee Wilson who can sometimes be overly dramatic, rather like an out-of-control Jimmy Witherspoon. Wide-ranging and occasionally scatting, Wilson is always an interesting singer. Leon Thomas is a very blues-orientated jazz singer who uses advanced scat-singing based on vocalese. He considers Joe Carroll and John Coltrane to be his major influences, although he shows signs of having absorbed much from bluesmen Arthur Prysock and B.B. King. Grover Washington and George Benson, while working in the jazz-funk idiom, veer more towards the pop world in their vocalising, just as they have with their instrumental work.

Searching among young singers for signs of jazz influences was once a rather hopeless task but in recent years it has become encouragingly easier.

Lorraine Feather is the daughter of Leonard Feather and hence grew up in a jazz-saturated atmosphere, albeit one possibly more intellectually-based than that which provided the formative background for most singers. She has a strong voice, a considerable range and, not surprisingly, given her family background, an extensive but selective and highly sophisticated repertoire.

Carole Leigh and Natalie Lamb continue the blues tradition of Bessie Smith into the 1980s, although black singers continue to dominate popular singing. Helen Geltzer works within the vaudeville tradition using jazz standards, as does the slightly more mature Bertice Reading. Such performers as Martha Reeves, Gladys Knight and Roberta Flack sing in the modern soul idiom but with the sonority of the classic blues singers. Fontella Bass came from a similar mould but now uses her gospel-influenced voice to dramatic effect with such avant-garde musicians as trumpeter Lester Bowie. Ex-Crusaders singer Randy Crawford has had a number of solo successes since leaving the group. All these singers have the quality of voice necessary to be comfortable within a jazz context.

Also working generally outside the jazz and blues scene, Ricky Lee Jones is clearly influenced by both forms and uses the blues structure especially with great success. Weslia Whitfield was opera-trained, and while this is usually a death-blow to anyone wanting to perform in jazz, she seems to have overcome the hurdle. An effortlessly elegant album, 'Lady Love', recorded in 1981, shows off her talent to perfection. Her expectedly excellent voice bends beautifully to such songs as *Fly Me To The Moon* and her interpretations of *You Go To My Head* and *Since I Fell For You* are quite superb.

Maria Muldaur makes free use of jazz-orientated material, singing in a light, sensual style. Her repertoire includes such songs as Carmichael's *Georgia On My Mind*, Ellington's *Prelude To A Kiss* and Don Redman's *Gee Baby Ain't I Good To You*. She also makes full use of jazz musicians in her accompanying groups, among them Seldon Powell (ts), Kenny Barron (p) and barrelhouse pianist Doctor John. Flora Purim and Tania Maria have gained many successes at jazz festivals around the world. Dorothy Donegan, a singer-pianist in the tradition of Cleo Brown, Nellie Lutcher and Rose Murphy, is a powerhouse performer who continues to delight audiences on both sides of the Atlantic with her exciting and stomping renditions of standards and blues songs.

In Great Britain, the National Youth Jazz Orchestra, in addition to being a proving ground for many young instrumentalists, has also produced a fine singer in Litsa Davies who demonstrates considerable flair in all her performances. When Litsa moved on, her place was taken by Helen Sorrell, who is already showing at least as much promise. Also working in Britain today is a young Caribbean-born Soul singer. Although much lighter-voiced than most of the noted

American Soul singers, Ruby Turner has many fine qualities and her future career could prove interesting, especially if she can negotiate the tricky course among pop-music's image-makers.

Another British singer is Carol Kidd who retired from singing when the 1960s trad scene faded. In the late 1970s she began working extensively but obscurely in clubs until a recent album, an engagement at Ronnie Scott's, and appearances on TV and radio brought her to the attention of the wider audience she deserves.

The mid-1980s also saw the forceful presence of Lena Horne on the stages of Broadway and London's West End. Although decidedly white-sounding in her Cotton Club days, her singing in her one-woman show displays a marked and deliberate 'blackening' of her sound. This is complemented by barely-concealed anger at the racism she has encountered during certain stages of her career.

So, there are survivors of a bygone age, there is the solid core of stylish mainstreamers, and there are encouraging signs of new-comers on the horizon – but where are the latterday giants of jazz singing? Perhaps the place to seek them is among that group of singers who have to struggle, as have so many jazz instrumentalists, against the imposition of the confining label: modernist.

Like all labels in jazz, or in any area of music and the arts in general, the term 'modernist' conjures up different things to different people. For some it is a term of approval, many use it contemptuously. In reality, it is meaningless. No doubt there were those who decried the stirring changes in Kansas City in the 1930s as being unacceptable modernism. What must be accepted, even if it is not liked by some, is that music is not a frozen moment in time captured on a gramophone record. Music is alive, and if it is to survive it has to change and adapt. There is no reason, of course, why the old ways cannot live alongside the new. Indeed, this coexistence is vital for the new needs the roots of the old.

Norma Winstone (1941–) is unmistakably a contemporary singer who often stretches the limits of jazz in her work. In much of her recorded output she uses her voice instrumentally rather than as a

Norma Winstone – unmistakably original.

vehicle for lyrics. This has led some to suspect that her range is limited but this is not so. Norma began singing while still a child and acknowledges that in her earlier years her voice suggested external influences. Nevertheless, none was consciously adopted. Her favourite singers were Lena Horne and Frank Sinatra, but she later took greater interest in Louis Armstrong, Ella Fitzgerald and Carmen McRae. It was, however, from jazz instrumentalists that she consciously drew most inspiration. In conversation with jazz writer Stan Woolley, she has cited Miles Davis, Eric Dolphy and, especially, John Coltrane. When she heard Coltrane she 'thought how fantastic it would be if one could develop one's voice somehow to the capacity that he had done with his instrument'. In Norma's work with Michael Garrick and Kenny Wheeler, among many of Britain's leading contemporary jazz musicians, her use of her voice as an instrument was further refined and developed, a task in which she was aided by her excellent pitch. Occasionally venturing into free form she continued to sing standards in a more orthodox manner, but it is wordless singing that established her reputation as one of the most original singers to appear in jazz in recent years.

Gifted with an amazing five-octave range, Ursula Dudziak has also chosen to use her voice instrumentally. Much of her material veers into jazz-rock fusion and she makes extensive use of electronics and, for many, this has placed her on the edge of the jazz world. Her musicianship is of the highest quality, however, and she represents a major force for change in jazz singing.

In the early-1960s Jeanne Lee, together with pianist Ran Blake, developed a unique, freely improvised, dual performance, blending voice and piano within a flexible discipline. The passage of time has not diminished the quality of her work, suggesting that its merits were much greater than was allowed a quarter-century ago. Annette Peacock showed early promise with an excellent first album, 'I'm the One', but her potential as a singer was never fully realised within the orthodox jazz world. In the 1960s she was highly successful, contributing material for Paul Bley. Her more recent vocal work has taken her first into fusion and then almost completely over that uncertain dividing line between jazz-rock and rock.

Sathima Bea Benjamin is a rarity among jazz artists in that she is South African–born. Since moving to America she has proved an

194

interesting singer and one not afraid to introduce statements of ideological belief into her work. She is clearly a singer of much potential, although her appeal to the wider audience may prove troublesome, given the disinclination of many to take polemic with their entertainment. If this is so, it will be unfortunate as she displays much promise and uses her strong voice and clear diction to generally good effect. It will, of course, be equally sad if she is obliged to jettison her convictions in order to succeed.

Al Jarreau sings a highly sophisticated form of vocalese within which can be discerned marked influences from many areas of jazz, together with numerous external influences. The range of influence has made him both hard to classify and more accessible to the wider audience for crossover music. He writes much of his own material, although his earlier career was centred on the West Coast nightclub scene where he sang standards and jazz classics. More commercially successful than most jazz singers, Jarreau is one of the few men around today who commands the wider audience of young people who have grown up more attuned to fusions in contemporary popular music.

Another young singer of similar appeal is Bobby McFerrin, whose astonishing vocal gymnastics and instrumental mimicry are proving enormously popular. His innovatory vocalese style is awash with superb technical skills. He has recorded with Weather Report and appeared at many festivals.

Abbey Lincoln first came to prominence in the 1950s with club dates and interesting albums, on one of which she was accompanied by Benny Carter. In the early 1960s she moved into the modern jazz scene and worked with pianist Thelonious Monk, and drummer Max Roach to whom she was married. With her husband she worked on a number of important compositions which reflect their joint involvement in black activism. Clearly influenced by Billie Holiday, Abbey Lincoln's singing voice is powerfully dramatic, a factor which enhances the political aspect of some of her work. In recent years she has been known by the name Aminata Moseka.

So, who are the giants? Of all modern singers in jazz two stand out above all others.

Sheila Jordan (1929–) was born in Pennsylvania's coal mining country and grew up in poverty. As a child Sheila sang all the time but there was little hope that it would come to anything until her mother (she never knew her father) took her to Detroit while she was still a young teenager. Almost at once Sheila began hearing the musician whose work changed her life: Charlie Parker. She began singing semi-professionally and, of necessity, worked extensively in black neighbourhoods and with black musicians, actions which led to criticism from other whites. By the time she was out of school she had decided on a career in music. With two others she formed a vocal trio, Skeeter, Mitch and Jean (she was Jean) and they sang Charlie Parker tunes, making up words to Bird's solos. In many respects this group was similar to the trio of Lambert, Hendricks and Ross who were not formed until a decade later. The trio even sang with Bird and she met up with her idol again when she moved to New York in the early 1950s. It was there that she married Parker's pianist, Duke Jordan and continued her schooling in modern music.

It was not until 1963 that Sheila made her first album which was followed by a European tour. Studies with Charles Mingus and Lennie Tristano extended her range but also tended to reduce her visibility by concentrating her into a small, commercially unpopular corner of jazz. To make matters worse, the 1960s was a time when jazz was undergoing one of its periodic blights. Nevertheless, an album she made with George Russell, 'Portrait of Sheila', gained critical approval but later works with Russell were less successful. Russell, an uncompromising musician, ignored commercialism in all his work. This was unfortunate for the development of Sheila's career as her interpretation of *You Are My Sunshine* on Russell's 'Outer Thoughts' album was a marvellously evocative piece.

In the mid-1960s she began singing jazz liturgies in church and continued recording, albeit for the benefit of a small, if devoted selection of admirers. It was not until the late 1970s that she began to reach a wider audience, although without having to sacrifice her deeply-rooted integrity. The audience had finally reached up to her, rather than requiring Sheila to reach down and compromise.

A dedicated and uncompromising jazz singer, she shows great harmonic perception in all her work and sings with marked originality. She chooses her repertoire with care and taste and is at her best when improvising on a good melodic line. A creative performer,

Sheila Jordan – dedicated perception.

Sheila Jordan is one of the finest singers to emerge from the bebop years.

Indeed, Sheila might well have been the leading exponent of the post-bop style of jazz singing were it not for the fact that she is a near-contemporary of Betty Carter.

Born in Flint, Michigan, Betty Carter (1930–), like Sheila Jordan, also started singing professionally in Detroit and in the mid-1940s was similarly attracted to the music of Charlie Parker. Her first important job was with Lionel Hampton in 1948 where she learned her music in the heat of one of the most dynamic of the big bands, and, indeed, one of the few that was left by this time. Betty's relationship with Hampton appears to have been one of armed neutrality. Oddly enough, Hampton seldom seemed comfortable with young, upcoming modern musicians yet never stopped hiring them. The list of instrumentalists who began with him before moving on to great things in modern jazz is seemingly endless. Hampton also gave a start to several singers of note, not least Dinah Washington. It was while she was with Hampton that Betty Carter picked up her nickname of Bebop Betty, a title apparently bestowed upon her somewhat disparagingly to reflect Hamp's disapproval of her style. Despite being fired periodically, this experience was calculated to separate women from girls. Only someone with Betty's strong, extrovert personality could have survived, let alone flourished.

In the 1950s Betty worked on the fringes of the r&b scene, appearing with Muddy Waters, Sonny Terry and Brownie McGhee and others, and for a few years at the start of the next decade she toured with Ray Charles. The 1960s proved as difficult for Betty as they had for Sheila Jordan and most other jazz artists. Trapped between the surge in popularity of Soul and the movement towards free-form music in jazz, she languished.

At the start of the 1970s she formed her own record company, determined to conduct her career as she wanted and without external influence or commercial consideration. By this time in her career, Betty was showing herself to be the ablest exponent of scat singing around, taking the form far beyond the sanitised popular variety offered by Ella Fitzgerald. Betty has stated that the greatest influences in her career were Charlie Parker and Sonny Rollins, both

Betty Carter – devastating attack.

saxophonists, and this is clearly demonstrated in all her singing, especially in her scatting. Her technique draws little from previous vocal traditions, yet there is a constant undercurrent of blues feeling even if, as on her *New Blues*, she reworks the form to startling effect.

In performance Betty Carter tends to favour the lower range of her voice, using it to stretch and bend melodies to her requirements. She improvises with enormous skill and ingenuity while never losing an aurally evident sense of humour. Understandably, lyrics tend to be treated with scant regard if they get in the way of what she wants the performance of a song to achieve. On such recordings as her album 'Betty Carter with the Audience' she takes this to extraordinary extremes with one tune, *Sounds*, most of which is wordless vocalese extending to more than twenty-five minutes. Her sheer inventive power is quite remarkable and it is difficult to think of many instrumentalists in jazz capable of sustaining interest for so long, let alone any other singer.

When faced with expendable lyrics, such as those on *My Favourite Things*, she dumps them unceremoniously and rips the tune off at breakneck tempo, dispelling forever any cloying memories of *The Sound Of Music*. *The Trolley Song* and *The Surrey With The Fringe On Top* are other tunes she chooses to take at a rate somewhat faster than the average trolley or surrey travels. Yet, when the spirit moves her, and it often does, Betty Carter can float leisurely through a lyrically inventive performance in a manner which imbues her material with superb qualities of musicianship. Monk's *'Round About Midnight* is an example, as is *I Cry Alone*.

In concert, Betty Carter is a dominating figure, striding the stage like a recently caged tiger and delivering her material with power and devastating attack. Indeed, her audiences need stamina much like that the lady herself possesses. The air of barely suppressed tension emanating from the singer soon spreads to her audience. This tension builds climactically throughout each of her shows, always to great, dramatic effect. At one such concert, in New York in 1979, she shared the bill with Sarah Vaughan and Eddie Jefferson. At the end of the evening the three joined forces for a scat 'contest' which proved to be a decidedly one-sided affair. Notwithstanding Sassy's undoubtedly superior vocal equipment, or Eddie's bop-singing expertise, they were wasted by the machine-gun attack of

Betty Carter who demonstrated her now unquestioned authority in this field.

The word 'great' is attached to innumerable artists throughout show business although, in reality, this often overstates their true worth. Among jazz instrumentalists there have been a few giants whose greatness transcends the boundaries of the form. Similarly, among jazz singers there have been few truly worthy of the term 'great' yet the countless good singers, unlike their instrumental counterparts, have been too readily disregarded although, ironically, it is they who reach the widest audience.

Perhaps the wide range of such singers, as revealed in this book, is at the core of their dismissal from serious consideration. From prison farms to glittering concert platforms, they have demonstrated their art. Sometimes they seem too crude, and at other times they are apparently too bland for informed critical assessment. Yet, the uncultured rawness of the country blues singer may conceal those same emotional depths that lie at the heart of all great jazz performances. The poised, skilled virtuoso who sings with effortless ease disguises the same dedication and determination displayed by the acknowledged jazz instrumentalists.

The purpose of this book has been to accord these singers their due, and to assess their merit in the world of jazz, and in relation to the wider world of popular music.

As to the future, on several occasions Betty Carter has declared that she despairs because no one is coming up to threaten her superiority. Given the huge number of excellent singers around today, her fears appear to be groundless but, on closer examination, it is clear what she means. Apart from her immediate contemporary, Sheila Jordan, and, possibly, such singers as Norma Winstone and Ursula Dudziak whose appeal has so far proved limited, none of the other singers performing today are innovators. Excellent as some undoubtedly are – Ernestine Anderson, Etta Jones, Carrie Smith, Mark Murphy, Mel Tormé, Helen Merrill, Anita O'Day, Carmen McRae, Sarah Vaughan, Ella Fitzgerald, Jimmy Witherspoon, Joe

Williams – none will reshape jazz singing, however much they might illuminate it today or influence their successors tomorrow.

It is in their influence that the hope for the future lies, for as young singers come along the jazz and blues background can still be imparted, even if only by experience once removed. The chance to learn as singer with a big band no longer exists; a singer can only rarely gain experience through working in clubs; all the old proving grounds are gone. But for those who want to learn, and clearly there are many that do, it will still be possible, provided that they are as dedicated as all the jazz singers of the past have been; and that artificial boundaries are discarded, as they have been in this book; and, also, provided that audiences are prepared to grant that there must be some movement with the times. It is false to expect that a jazz singer emerging in the 1980s will sound like the singers of the 1950s, let alone like those of even earlier decades.

Jazz and the blues have always been close to the ground, reflecting the times in which the music was performed, speaking to the people in the langauge of the day. That is how jazz in the future must be performed. Of course, there are pessimists around who question whether or not jazz has a future, but people have been asking that same question for the past eighty years. There is no reason to suppose they will stop now, anymore than there is real reason to suppose that jazz will end. And if jazz never ends, then neither will jazz singing, even in the post-industrial age we are assured is looming towards us. In the beginning was song; very possibly that will be all that remains when the rest is ashes.

Bibliography

Albertson, Chris: *Bessie*. London: Barrie & Jenkins. 1972.

Balliett, Whitney: *American Singers*. New York: OUP. 1979.

Broughton, Viv: *Black Gospel*. Poole: Blandford. 1985.

Charters, Samuel B: *The Country Blues*. New York: Michael Joseph. 1959.

Charters, Samuel B. and Kunstadt, Leonard: *Jazz: A History Of The New York Scene*. New York: Doubleday. 1962.

Chilton, John: *Billie's Blues*. London: Quartet. 1977.

Chilton, John: *Who's Who Of Jazz*. London: Chilton. 1972.

Collier, James Lincoln: *Louis Armstrong*. London: Pan. 1985.

Dahl, Linda: *Stormy Weather*. London: Quartet. 1984.

Dixon, R.M.W. and Godrich, J.: *Recording The Blues*. London: Studio Vista. 1970.

Ellison, Ralph: *Shadow And Act*. New York: Vintage. 1972.

Ewen, David: *All The Years Of American Popular Song*. Englewood Cliffs, NJ: Prentice-Hall. 1977.

Gammond, Peter ed.: *The Decca Book Of Jazz*. London: Muller 1958.

Giddins, Gary: *Riding On A Blue Note*. New York: OUP. 1981.

Gillett, Charlie: *The Sound Of The City*. London: Sphere. 1971.

Harris, Sheldon: *Blues Who's Who*. New York: Da Capo. 1979.

Hughes, Langston: *The Big Sea*. New York: Knopf. 1940.

Kimball, Robert and Bolcam, William: *Reminiscing With Sissle And Blake*. New York: Viking Press. 1973.

O'Day, Anita with Eells, George: *High Times Hard Times*. London: Corgi. 1983.

Oliver, Paul: *The Story Of The Blues*. London: Barrie & Jenkins. 1978.

Ostransky, Leroy: *Jazz City*. Englewood Cliffs, NJ: Prentice-Hall. 1978.

Placksin, Sally: *American Women In Jazz*. New York: Wideview. 1982.

Priestley, Brian: 'Discourse', *Jazz Journal International*, November 1977.

Roberts, John Storm: *Black Music Of Two Worlds*. London: Allen Lane. 1973.

Shaw, Arnold: *Honkers And Shouters: The Golden Years Of Rhythm & Blues*. New York: Macmillan. 1978.

Southern, Eileen: *The Music Of Black Americans: A History*. New York: Norton. 1971.

Stearns, Marshall and Stearns, Jean: *Jazz Dance: The Story Of American Vernacular Dance*. New York: Schirmer 1964.

Stewart-Baxter, Derrick: *Ma Rainey And The Classic Blues Singers*. London: Studio Vista. 1970.

Stewart-Baxter, Derrick: 'Blues & Views', *Jazz Journal*, various issues 1974–76.

Van Vechten, Carl: 'Bessie Smith', *Jazz Record*, September 1947.

Waters, Ethel: *His Eye Is On The Sparrow*. London: W.H. Allen. 1951.

White, John: 'Veiled Testimony' *Journal Of American Studies*, Vol. 17, No. 2, 1983.

Wilder, Alec: *American Popular Song*. New York: OUP. 1972.

Woolley, Stan: 'Norma Winstone', *Jazz Journal*, July 1975.

(The passages on Mildred Bailey, Helen Humes and Lee Wiley appeared in different form in *Jazz Journal*.)

Selected Recordings

The following list of records is intended only as a guide to readers. Everyone familiar with the vagaries of the jazz record market will be aware that many items of American, Japanese or European origin may be difficult to obtain other than from specialist shops. Wherever possible recent issues are listed but in some instances it will be necessary to settle for second-hand. Good hunting!

Lorez Alexandria
Discovery DS 800 *A Woman Knows*

Ernestine Anderson
Concord CJ 54 *Live From Concord To London*
Concord CJ 147 *Never Make Your Move Too Soon*
Concord CJ 263 *When The Sun Goes Down*

Pink Anderson
Original Blues Classics OBC 504 *Carolina Blues Man, Vol. 1*

Louis Armstrong
MCA Coral CP 1 *Swing That Music*
World Records SH 404, 5, 6, 7 *The LA Legend*
CBS 52067 *LA Plays W.C. Handy*
RCA PM 45374 *LA At Town Hall*
Columbia ML 4383, 4, 5 *The LA Story, Vol. 1, 2, 3*

Mildred Bailey
Regent 6032 *Me And The Blues*
Monmouth-Evergreen 6814 *All Of Me*
CBS JC3L22 *MB: Her Greatest Performances 1929–1946, Vol. 1, 2, 3*

Pearl Bailey
MCA MCL 1744 *Hello Pearlie Mae*

Sathima Bea Benjamin
Ekapa EK 003 *Memories And Dreams*

Blind Blake
Matchbox MSE 1003 *BB, 1926–29*

Bobby Bland
Ace CH 32 *Blues In The Night*

Connee Boswell
Biograph C3 *Boswell Sisters*
Victor RD 27017 *CB And The Original Memphis Five In Hi-Fi*
MCA MCL 1689 *Sand In My Shoes*
Decca DL 8356 *Connee*

Dardanelle Breckenridge
Stash ST 217 *The Colours Of My Life*

Big Bill Broonzy
Vogue 512510 *Feelin' Low Down*

Charles Brown
Route 66 KIX 5 *CB And Johnny Moore's Three Blazers*
Route 66 KIX 17 *Race Track Blues*

Gabriel Brown
Flyright 591 *GB, 1943–45*

Roy Brown
Route 66 KIX 26 *I Feel That Young Man's Rhythm*

Ruth Brown
Blue Note LA 392 *Thad Jones/Mel Lewis*
Skye SK 13 *Black Is Brown*
Charly CRB 1069 *Rockin' With Ruth*

Jackie Cain & Roy Kral
Brunswick BL 54025 *Here's Charlie*
Concord CJ 149 *East Of Suez*

Blanche Calloway
Raretone RTR 24005

Cab Calloway
RCA NL 89560 *1931–34 And 1949* (with Blanche Calloway and Billy Banks)
Living Era AJA 5013 *Kicking The Gong Around*

Una Mae Carlisle/Savannah Churchill
Harlequin HQ 2002 *UMC-& SC 1944*

Leroy Carr
Magpie PY 4407 *LC 1930–35*

Wynona Carr
Ace CH 130 *Hit That Jive Jack!*

Betty Carter
Bet-Car MK 1001 *BC*
Bet-Car MK 1002 *BC*
Bet-Car MK 1003 *The Audience With BC*
Bet-Car MK 1004 *Whatever Happened To Love?*
UA UAS 5639 *Inside BC*
ABC Impulse 9321 *What A Little Moonlight Can Do*

Jeannie Cheatham
Concord CJ 258 *Sweet Baby Blues*

June Christy
Capitol T 1202 *Those Kenton Days*
Capitol CAPS 26 0051 1 *This Is JC*
Swing House SWH 20 *June Time*

Rosemary Clooney
Concord CJ 47 *Everything's Coming Up Rosie*
Capitol CAPS 1017 *That Travellin' Two-Beat* (with Bing Crosby)

Nat 'King' Cole
MCA 204 868 *In The Beginning*

Chris Connor
Progressive Jazz 7028 *Sweet And Swinging*
Bethlehem BTM 6823 *CC Sings Lullabies Of Birdland*

Ida Cox
Fountain FB 301, 4 *IC, Vol. 1, 2*
Riverside RLP 147 *The Moanin' And Groanin' Blues*
Rosetta RR 1304 *Wild Women Don't Have The Blues*

Bing Crosby
Joker SM 3053 *The Jazzin' BC*
Living Era AJA 5005 *Bix 'n' Bing*

Thomas A. Dorsey
Yazoo L 1041 *Georgia Tom Dorsey*

Ursula Dudziak
Inner City 1066 *Future Talk*

Champion Jack Dupree
Paris C 3303 *Live 1979*

Billy Eckstine
RCA Savoy WC 70522 *Mr B And The Band*

Ella Fitzgerald
CBS 88621 *Newport Jazz Festival Live At Carnegie Hall*
Verve 821.554.1 *At The Chicago Opera House*
Verve VE2.2507 *Porgy And Bess* (with Louis Armstrong)
Verve CLP 1146, 7 *Ella and Louis Again, Vol. 1, 2* (with Louis
    Armstrong)
Jazz Live BLJ 8010 *At the Southland Of Boston, 1939*
Joker SM 3054 *The Best Years*
Pablo 2310 702 *Take Love Easy*

Aretha Franklin
Atlantic SD 8139 *I Never Loved A Man*
Columbia CS 8879 *Laughing On The Outside*
CBS 22112 *The Legendary Queen Of Soul*

Dave Frishberg
Omnisound Jazz N 1040 *The DF Songbook*
Fantasy F9638 *Live At Vine Street.*

Lowell Fulson
United US 7768 *Let's Get Stoned*

Slim Gaillard
Hep HEP 6 *Macvoutie* (also Leo Watson & Harry Gibson)
Folklyric 9038 *Cement Mixer*

Odetta Gordon
Original Blues Classics OBC 509 *Odetta And The Blues*

Lil Green
Victor LP V574 *Romance In The Dark*

Adelaide Hall
Decca RFL 3 *There Goes That Song Again*
Collectors Items CI 011 *Strange As It Seems* (with Art Tatum)

Annette Hanshaw
Fountain FV 201, 2 *AH, Vol. 1, 2*

Wynonie Harris
Route 66 KIX 3 *Mr Blues Comin' To Town*

Billie Holiday
Columbia C3I21 *BH: The Golden Years, Vol. I, II, III*
Columbia PG 32121, 4, 7 *The BH Story, Vol. I, II, III*
Columbia CS 8048 *Lady In Satin*
Verve V 8026 *Songs For Torching*
Verve V 8257 *Songs For Distingué Lovers*

Pug Horton
Bodeswell BW 102 *Don't Go Away*

Howling Wolf
Cleo CL 003683 *I Am The Wolf*

Helen Humes
Black Lion BLP 30167 *HH*
Muse MR 5217 *HH & The Muse All Stars*
Black & Blue 33050 *Helen Comes Back*
Black & Blue 33083 *Sneaking Around*
Whiskey, Women, and ... KM 701 *Be-Baba-Leba*

Alberta Hunter
Columbia JS 355 *Remember My Name*
Columbia FC 37691 *The Glory Of AH*
DRG SL 5195 *The Legendary AH: The London Sessions, 1934*
Stash ST 115 *Classic AH*

International Sweethearts of Rhythm
Rosetta RR 1312 *Hot Big Band*

Mahalia Jackson
Columbia CS 8804 *MJ: Greatest Hits*
Vogue 600061 *In The Upper Room*

Elmore James
Blue Moon BMLP 008 *Red Hot Blues*

Etta James
Charly CH 73 *Tuff Lover*
Quicksilver QS 5014 *Red Hot And Live*

Al Jarreau
WEA International U 0070 *Jarreau*

Frankie Jaxon
Collectors Items CI 013 *FJ And Tampa Red's Hokum Jug Band*
Collectors Items CI 014 *Can't You Wait Till You Get Home*

Lonnie Johnson
Blues Boy BB 300 *The Originator Of Modern Guitar Blues*
Queen-disc QU 043 *It Feels Good*
Swaggie S 1225 *The Blues Of LJ*

Merline Johnson
Earl Archives BD 601 *The Yas Yas Girl, 1938–1941*

Etta Jones
Muse 5099 *Ms Jones To You*
Muse 5214 *Save Your Love For Me*

Louis Jordan
MCA MCA 274 *LJ Greatest Hits*
MCA MCL 1631 *The Best of LJ*
Charly CDY 7 *Jivin' With Jordan*

Charly CRB 1048 *Look Out!*

Sheila Jordan
Milestone M 47027 *Outer Thoughts*
Steeplechase SCS 1081 *Sheila*
Wave LP 1 *Looking Out*
ECM 1-1159 *Playground*
Black Saint BRS 0023 *Free To Dance*
Vista RCA TLP1-1082 *Perdas De Fogu*

Carol Kidd
Aloi AKH 003 *CK*

B.B. King
Charly CH 86 *BBK Live At The Regal*

Teddi King
Inner City 1044 *This Is New*

Karin Krog
Spotlite SPJ LP 22 *I Remember You*
Storyville SLP 4045 *Some Other Spring*

Cleo Laine
Black Lion 162028

Lambert, Hendricks & Ross
Columbia C 32911 *Best Of LH&R*

Barbara Lea
Audiophile AP 86 *A Woman In Love*

Huddie Ledbetter
Playboy PB 119 *Leadbelly*

Julia Lee
Juke Box Lil JB 603 *Ugly Papa, 1945–57*

Peggy Lee
Jasmine JASM 1026 *Black Coffee*
Jasmine JASM 1032 *Dream Street*
MCA MCL 1832 *The Best Of PL*
CBS 32417 *PL Sings With Benny Goodman*

Smiley Lewis
KC KC 102 *Hook Line And Sinker*

Abbey Lincoln
Riverside RLP 12–251 *That's Him*

Little Willie Littlefield
Paris PLB 228508 *Paris Street Lights*

Nellie Lutcher
Capitol EG 2604 791 *Real Gone Gal*

Susannah McCorkle
Black Lion BLP 12169 *The Quality Of Mercer*
Inner City 1131 *The Songs Of Yip Harburg*
World Records WRS 1001 *There Will Never Be Another You*

Bobby McFerrin
Elektra K 52387 *BMcF*

Carmen McRae
Concord CJ 128 *Two For The Road*
Concord CJ 189 *Heat Wave*
Kingdom Jazz Gate 7001 *Live At Bubba's, 1981*
Main MRL 387 *CM In Person*
Main MRL 403 *Live And Doin' It*

Brownie McGhee
Original Blues Classics OBC 507 *Brownie's Blues*

Memphis Slim
Original Blues Classics OBC 509 *All Kinds Of Blues*

Mabel Mercer
Audiophone 161/2 *Echoes of My Life, Vol. I, II*

Helen Merrill
Spotlite SPJLP 12 *A Shade Of Difference*
Catalyst 7903 *HM Sings & Swings*

Roy Milton
United US *The Great RM, Vol. 1*
Juke Box Lil JB 600 *Grandfather Of R&B 1945–49*

Jelly Roll Morton
RCA CL 43291 *The Best Of JRM*
Joy JOY 265 *I'm A Winin' Boy*

Mark Murphy
Muse 5041 *Mark II*
Muse 5078 *MM Sings*
Muse 5215 *Satisfaction Guaranteed*

Anita O'Day
CBS Sony 20 AP *AO'D Sings With Gene Krupa*
Verve MV 2526 *An Evening With AO'D*
Verve MGV 2000 *Anita*
Verve MGV 2157 *Travelin' Light*
Emily 9579 *Live In Tokyo*
Emily ER 13081 *Angel Eyes*

Esther Phillips
Atlantic ATL 50521 *Confessin' The Blues*

Ma Rainey
Milestone MLP 2001 *Immortal MR*
Milestone M47021 *MR* (2 Vol.)
Biograph 12001 *Blues The World Forgot, Vol. I*
Biograph 12011 *Oh My Babe Blues, Vol. II*
Biograph 12032 *Queen Of The Blues, Vol. III*

Jimmy Rushing
Master Jazz MJR 8104 *Gee, Baby, Ain't I Good To You?*
Master Jazz MJR 8120 *Who Was It Sang That Song?*
RCA SF 8234 *The You And Me That Used To Be*
Vanguard VRS 8518 *Goin' To Chicago*
Vogue VJD 556 *The Essential JR*
Philips B 07235 L *The Jazz Odyssey Of JR*

Nina Simone
Festival 189 *A Portrait Of NS*

Bessie Smith
Columbia CL 855, 6, 7 *Bessie Smith Story, Vol. I, II, III*
CBS 66258 *The World's Greatest Blues Singer*

CBS 66262 *Any Woman's Blues*
CBS 66273 *Empty Bed Blues*
CBS 66264 *The Empress*
CBS 67232 *Nobody's Blues But Mine*

Carrie Smith
Audiophile AP164 *Fine And Mellow.*
Black & Blue 33 103 *Do Your Duty*
West 54 WLW 8002 *CS.*

Keely Smith
Reprise P 7731 *KS*

Valaida Snow
Rosetta RR 1305 *Hot Snow: Queen Of The Trumpet Sings & Swings*
World Records SH 354 *Swing Is The Thing*

The Spirits of Rhythm
JSP 1088 *Rhythm Personified*

Victoria Spivey
Spivey 1001 *Victoria And Her Blues*
Spivey 2001 *The VS Recorded Legacy Of The Blues*

Kay Starr
Capitol CAPS 1867481 *Jazz Singer*

Maxine Sullivan
Stash ST 244 *The Great Songs From The Cotton Club*
Monmouth-Evergreen MES 6919 *Close As Pages In A Book*
Monmouth-Evergreen MES 7038 *Shakespeare*
Kenneth KS 2052 *The Queen And Her Swedish Jazz All Stars*

Sunnyland Slim
Flyright LP 566 *Classic Early 50s Chicago Blues*

Jack Teagarden
Queen-disc QU 012 *JT*
Queen-disc QU 027 *JT*
Musi-disc CV 1073 *Memorial*
Teagarden 11221 *That Kid From Texas!*

Sister Rosetta Tharpe
Savoy SGL 7029 *The Best Of SRT (2 Vol.)*

Big Mama Thornton
Arhoolie F 1028 *Big Mama In Europe*
Arhoolie F 1032 *BMT And The Chicago Blues Band*

Mel Tormé
Affinity AFF 100 *Live At The Crescendo*
Affinity AFF 107 *MT Sings Astaire*
Affinity AFF 138 *It's A Blue World*

Joe Turner
Atlantic 1234 *The Boss Of The Blues*
Atlantic LT 2-K 15205 *Big Joe Rides Again*
Pablo 2310 709 *The Bosses*
Muse 5293 *Blues Train*
Savoy SJL 2223 *Have No Fear, Big Joe Is Here*

Sarah Vaughan
Pablo 2312 137 *Crazy & Mixed Up*
Pablo 2312 116 *Ellington Song Book, Vol. 2*
Discovery MVS 2002 *The Man I Love*
Reactivation JR 109 *SV, Vol. 1*
Bulldog BDL 1009 *Tenderly*

Eddie 'Cleanhead' Vinson
JSP 1012 *Fun In London*

T-Bone Walker
Charly CR 30144 *Stormy Monday Blues*

Fats Waller
EMI World Records SHB 29 *FW In London*
RCA Camden CDN 131 *The Real FW*
RCA FATS COF 1 *Complete Recordings, Vol. 1–10*

Dinah Washington
Trip 5500 *DW Jams With Clifford Brown*
Trip 5516 *After Hours*
Trip 5524 *Tears And Laughter*
Saga ERO 8070 *Back To The Blues*
Mercury 6641 573 *The Jazz Sides*
Fontana SFL 13073 *The Original Soul Sister, Queen Of The Blues*
Emarcy 818 930–1 *The Fats Waller Songbook*
Rosetta RR 1313 *Wise Woman Blues*

Ethel Waters
Biograph BLP 12022 *EW: 1921–24*
Biograph BLP 12026 *EW: 1921–27*
RCA 741 067 *EW: 1938–39*
Monmouth-Evergreen MES 6812 *Miss EW*
Word 8044 *His Eye Is On The Sparrow*
CSP P 2792 *On Stage And Screen*
Mercury MG 2005 *The Favourite Songs Of EW*

Muddy Waters
Vogue 515039 *MW At Newport 1960*
Cleo CL 0014983 *Mississippi*

Katie Webster
Arhoolie 1094 *You Know That's Right*

Georgia White
Rosetta RR 1307 *GW Sings And Plays The Blues*

Margaret Whiting
Audiophile AP 152 *Too Marvellous For Words*

Lee Wiley
Monmouth-Evergreen MES 6807 *LW Sings Rodgers & Hart and Harold Arlen*
Monmouth-Evergreen MES 7034E *LW Sings Gershwin And Porter*
Monmouth-Evergreen MES 7041 *Back Home Again*
RIC 2002 *The One And Only LW*
Ember CJS 829 *I've Got The World On A String!*

Joe Williams
Vogue VJD 553 *Every Day I Have The Blues*

Sonny Boy Williamson
Arhoolie 2020 *King Biscuit Time*

Jackie Wilson
Ace CH 125 *Reet Petite*

Edith Wilson
Fountain FB 302 *EW And Johnny Dunn's Jazz Hounds*

Norma Winstone
Argo ZDA 148 *Edge Of Time*

Jimmy Witherspoon
Vogue 500091 *Olympia Concert*
United US 7715 *A Spoonful Of Blues*
JSP 1032 *Big Blues*

Compilations By Various Artists

Spivey LP 1001 *Buddy Tate Invites You To Dig A Basket Of Blues* (inc. Victoria Spivey, Lucille Hegamin, Hannah Sylvester)

EMI World Records SH 265 *Harlem Comes To London* (inc. Valaida Snow, Lavaida Carter, Elisabeth Welch, Adelaide Hall)

Arhoolie/Blues Classics BC 26 *When Women Sang The Blues* (inc. Lillian Glinn, Chippie Hill, Memphis Minnie)

Savoy SJL 2233 *Ladies Sing The Blues* (2 Vol.) (inc. Viola Wells, Little Esther, Albinia Jones, Linda Hopkins)

Victor/RCA LPV 534 *Women of the Blues* (inc. Alberta Hunter, Mamie Smith, Victoria Spivey, Sippie Wallace)

Stash 117 *Streetwalking Blues* (inc. Clara Smith, Billie Pierce, Georgia White, Lucille Bogan)

Columbia DC 36811 (inc. Billie Holiday, Lena Horne, Sarah Vaughan)

Design 238 (inc. Ivie Anderson, Pearl Bailey, Rose Murphy)

MCA MCLD 614 *Black Gospel* (inc. Rosetta Tharpe, Clara Ward)

Magpie PY 4412 *Big Four 1933–41* (Little Brother Montgomery, Walter Davis, Roosevelt Sykes, Springback James)

Jitterbug 84121, 2 *Jivin' Girls, Vol. 1, 2* (inc. Roberta May, Stella Johnson, Annie Laurie, Margaret Whiting, Varetta Dillard)

Rosetta RR 1300 *Mean Mothers*

Rosetta RR 1301 *Women's Railroad Blues*

Rosetta RR 1302 *Red White And Blues*

Rosetta RR 1303 *Piano Singer's Blues*

Rosetta RR 1306 *Big Mama's*

Rosetta RR 1308 *Super Sisters*

Rosetta RR 1309 *Boogie Blues*

Rosetta RR 1311 *Sweet Petunias*

Spotlite SPJ 135 *Cool Whalin'* (inc. Joe Carroll, Babs Gonzales, Eddie Jefferson)

RCA NL 89276 *Memphis Blues* (inc. Memphis Minnie, Furry Lewis)

Index

Some pseudonyms have been cross-referenced, e.g. Memphis Slim and Chatman, Peter 'Memphis Slim'. Where an artist is almost exclusively known by a pseudonym there is no cross-reference but the surname (if known) appears in parantheses, e.g. Laughing Charlie (Hicks).
Page numbers of illustrations are printed in *italics*.

219

220